Dark Digital Histories

Shah Rukh

Published by Shah Rukh, 2024.

DARK DIGITAL HISTORIES

First edition. June 12, 2024.

ISBN: 979-8224775071

Written by Shah Rukh.

Table of Contents

Prologue

In the shadows of the digital realm, where binary code reigns supreme and firewalls stand as the sentinels of secrets, a parallel universe thrives—one of invisible heists, silent invasions, and meticulously orchestrated attacks. Welcome to "Dark Digital Histories," a chronicle of the most significant cybercrimes that have shaped the landscape of our interconnected world.

As technology has advanced, so too has the sophistication of those who seek to exploit it. The internet, once a nascent network of academic exchange, has evolved into a global infrastructure critical to every facet of modern life. Yet, with this progress comes vulnerability. The very systems designed to enhance our lives and secure our information have become targets for an array of cybercriminals, from lone hackers and hacktivist collectives to state-sponsored agents.

The stories within these pages are not mere tales of theft and disruption. They are narratives that reveal the intricate dance between those who defend the sanctity of data and those who seek to corrupt it. They expose the weaknesses in our digital armor and remind us of the ever-present need for vigilance and innovation in cybersecurity.

From the early days of the Morris Worm, which demonstrated the destructive potential of self-replicating code, to the sophisticated espionage operations of state actors, this book delves into the milestones that have defined the dark side of digital history. You will encounter infamous figures like Kevin Mitnick, whose exploits in the 1990s set the stage for modern hacking culture, and the relentless march of botnets and ransomware that have paralyzed infrastructure and extorted billions.

Each chapter unfolds a saga of technological ingenuity and criminal audacity. These are not just stories of breaches and losses but also of the human spirit—of those who battle in the trenches of cybersecurity, striving to outmaneuver and outthink their adversaries.

"Dark Digital Histories" serves as both a cautionary tale and a tribute to the resilience and resourcefulness of those who stand guard over our digital lives.

As you embark on this journey through the annals of cybercrime, may you gain a deeper understanding of the complexities and challenges that define our digital age. The battle for cyberspace is ongoing, and these histories remind us that in the ever-evolving world of technology, the shadows are always shifting, and the next chapter is only a keystroke away.

Chapter 1: Morris Worm

The Morris Worm, unleashed on November 2, 1988, represents one of the earliest and most significant instances of cybercrime, marking a pivotal moment in the history of the internet. Created by Robert Tappan Morris, a graduate student at Cornell University, this self-replicating computer program was intended to gauge the size of the nascent internet. However, it inadvertently caused widespread disruption, highlighting vulnerabilities in computer networks and sparking discussions about cybersecurity and ethical computing.

The worm exploited known vulnerabilities in Unix systems, specifically targeting flaws in the sendmail program, the Finger protocol, and weak passwords. Sendmail, a mail transfer agent, was particularly susceptible due to its widespread use and the lack of security measures inherent in early network protocols. The Finger protocol, which provided information about users logged into a network, was also exploited to gain unauthorized access. Additionally, the worm attempted to break into systems using a dictionary attack on weak passwords, highlighting the poor password hygiene prevalent at the time.

Once a system was infected, the worm would replicate itself and attempt to spread to other machines. It was designed with mechanisms to prevent multiple infections of the same machine; however, a flaw in the worm's code caused it to replicate excessively, even on already infected systems. This led to a significant slowdown in network performance and, in some cases, caused systems to crash. The self-replicating nature of the worm, combined with its rapid spread, resulted in approximately 6,000 computers being affected within hours, a substantial portion of the internet at the time.

The immediate impact of the Morris Worm was profound. Systems administrators across the United States scrambled to identify the source of the disruption and mitigate its effects. The worm's presence was first noticed by system operators at the Massachusetts Institute of Technology, who observed unusual system behavior and network traffic. As the worm spread, it overloaded processors and consumed system memory, rendering many computers unusable. Efforts to contain the worm involved disconnecting infected systems from the network, isolating segments of the internet, and developing patches to close the exploited vulnerabilities.

The response to the Morris Worm also marked a significant moment in the collaborative efforts of the internet community. Researchers and administrators shared information and strategies in real-time, showcasing the cooperative spirit that underpinned the early internet. This incident underscored the importance of timely communication and the sharing of technical knowledge to address widespread cyber threats. It also led to the creation of the first Computer Emergency Response Team (CERT) at Carnegie Mellon University, which became a model for similar organizations worldwide. CERT's establishment was a direct response to the worm, aimed at improving coordination and response to future cybersecurity incidents.

Legally, the Morris Worm case was groundbreaking. Robert Morris was prosecuted under the Computer Fraud and Abuse Act (CFAA), a relatively new piece of legislation at the time. In 1990, Morris was convicted of violating the CFAA, making him the first person to be convicted under this law. He was sentenced to three years of probation, 400 hours of community service, and a fine of $10,050. This case set important legal precedents and highlighted the need for clearer definitions and regulations regarding unauthorized computer access and activities. The prosecution of Morris underscored the legal system's evolving approach to cybercrime, balancing the need for deterrence with considerations of intent and the nascent state of cybersecurity law.

The legacy of the Morris Worm extends beyond its immediate impact. It served as a wake-up call to the potential dangers of interconnected systems and the ease with which malicious code could spread. This incident prompted a reevaluation of network security practices and accelerated the development of more robust security measures. The worm highlighted the necessity for regular software updates, stronger password policies, and the implementation of more sophisticated intrusion detection systems. It also underscored the importance of ethical considerations in programming and the unintended consequences that could arise from seemingly benign actions.

In academia, the Morris Worm became a case study in computer science and cybersecurity courses, illustrating both the technical aspects of network security and the ethical responsibilities of computer scientists. It demonstrated the critical need for responsible disclosure of vulnerabilities and the potential repercussions of experimental code released into operational environments. The incident also encouraged a generation of researchers and practitioners to focus on improving cybersecurity, laying the groundwork for many of the advances and best practices in use today.

Moreover, the Morris Worm influenced public perception of cybersecurity. It was one of the first times the general public became aware of the vulnerabilities inherent in computer networks. Media coverage of the incident brought attention to the importance of cybersecurity and the potential for widespread disruption caused by relatively simple exploits. This increased awareness among users, businesses, and policymakers, contributing to the growing emphasis on securing digital infrastructure as an essential component of national security and economic stability.

In the years following the Morris Worm, cybersecurity evolved significantly. The incident spurred advancements in antivirus software, firewalls, and network monitoring tools. Organizations began to prioritize security in their IT strategies, investing in both technology and personnel to protect their systems from similar threats. The worm also influenced the development of cybersecurity policies and legislation, shaping the regulatory landscape that governs digital activities today.

Chapter 2: Kevin Mitnick

Kevin Mitnick, a name synonymous with the early days of hacking, became one of the most infamous figures in cybercrime during the 1990s. His activities and subsequent pursuit by law enforcement highlighted both the vulnerabilities of burgeoning digital infrastructures and the evolving landscape of cybersecurity. Mitnick's story is a complex narrative of curiosity, technical skill, and ethical ambiguity, underscored by a cat-and-mouse game with authorities that captured the public's imagination and led to significant changes in cybercrime legislation and awareness.

Mitnick's journey into the world of hacking began at a young age. Growing up in Los Angeles, he developed an early fascination with technology and telecommunications systems. His first notable exploit occurred while he was still a teenager, when he successfully manipulated the Los Angeles public bus system to get free rides using unused transfer slips. This initial taste of hacking's potential led him to explore more sophisticated targets, eventually moving on to computer systems.

By the early 1980s, Mitnick had become proficient in gaining unauthorized access to computer networks. He famously broke into the North American Air Defense Command (NORAD) computer system, an incident that allegedly inspired the 1983 film "WarGames." Although this specific claim is contentious, it underscored the growing concern about the security of critical systems. Mitnick's exploits during this period earned him the attention of law enforcement, resulting in his first arrest in 1981 for stealing computer manuals from Pacific Bell.

Despite legal troubles, Mitnick's activities only escalated. Throughout the late 1980s and early 1990s, he embarked on a hacking spree that targeted some of the largest corporations in the United States, including Digital Equipment Corporation (DEC), Motorola, Nokia, and Sun Microsystems. His methods were diverse and sophisticated, involving social engineering, where he manipulated individuals into divulging confidential information, and technical exploits that took advantage of software vulnerabilities.

One of Mitnick's most notable techniques was "phone phreaking," a form of hacking that exploited the telephone network to make free calls and eavesdrop on communications. This practice allowed him to stay ahead of law enforcement by constantly changing locations and communicating covertly. Mitnick's ability to blend social engineering with technical prowess made him a particularly elusive target for authorities.

In 1989, Mitnick was arrested for hacking into DEC's computer network and stealing software. He was sentenced to a year in prison and three years of supervised release. However, Mitnick violated his probation and went on the run, leading to one of the most extensive and publicized manhunts in cybercrime history. For over two years, Mitnick evaded capture, using his hacking skills to stay hidden and continue his activities. During this time, he accessed thousands of computers, stealing valuable information, including proprietary software and credit card numbers.

Mitnick's evasion of law enforcement ended in 1995, when he was finally apprehended by the FBI with the assistance of Tsutomu Shimomura, a computer security expert whom Mitnick had antagonized by hacking into his systems. This high-profile capture took place in Raleigh, North Carolina, and was the culmination of intense investigative efforts. Mitnick's arrest was met with significant media coverage, highlighting both his notoriety and the growing public interest in hacking and cybersecurity.

The legal proceedings against Mitnick were equally high-profile. He was charged with multiple counts of wire fraud, computer fraud, and illegal interception of communications. The prosecution portrayed him as a highly dangerous individual who caused millions of dollars in damages through his activities. Mitnick, in his defense, argued that his actions were motivated more by curiosity and the challenge of overcoming security measures than by any intent to cause harm or profit financially.

In 1999, Mitnick reached a plea agreement, pleading guilty to seven counts of fraud and agreeing to serve 46 months in prison, with an additional 22 months for violating the terms of his supervised release. His sentence also included a prohibition on profiting from his story through books or films for seven years. Mitnick's imprisonment was a significant moment in the history of cybercrime, as it highlighted the serious legal consequences of hacking and the importance of cybersecurity.

Mitnick's release from prison in 2000 marked a new chapter in his life. He transitioned from notorious hacker to a cybersecurity consultant, leveraging his extensive knowledge of system vulnerabilities to help organizations protect against the very types of attacks he once perpetrated. He authored several books, including "The Art of Deception" and "The Art of Intrusion," where he detailed his exploits and provided insights into the techniques of social engineering and hacking.

The impact of Kevin Mitnick's case on the field of cybersecurity cannot be overstated. His actions exposed significant weaknesses in computer systems and networks, prompting organizations to invest more heavily in security measures. His story also contributed to a broader understanding of the importance of cybersecurity, influencing both public perception and policy. The Mitnick case underscored the need for improved cybersecurity education and training, as well as more robust legal frameworks to address the complexities of cybercrime.

Moreover, Mitnick's transformation from hacker to security consultant exemplifies the potential for individuals with deep technical skills to contribute positively to the field of cybersecurity. His experience highlighted the value of understanding the mindset and techniques of attackers in order to develop effective defenses. This perspective has influenced the development of "ethical hacking" and the growing practice of hiring former hackers to test and improve organizational security.

Kevin Mitnick's legacy is a testament to the evolving nature of cybercrime and cybersecurity. His story is a reminder of the rapid pace of technological change and the ongoing challenges in securing digital environments. As cyber threats continue to grow in sophistication and scale, the lessons from Mitnick's exploits remain relevant, emphasizing the importance of vigilance, innovation, and collaboration in the fight against cybercrime. His journey from notorious hacker to respected security expert underscores the complex and often paradoxical relationship between criminal activity and technological advancement in the digital age.

Chapter 3: Mafiaboy

In February 2000, the digital world was rocked by a series of unprecedented and highly disruptive cyberattacks orchestrated by a teenage hacker known as "Mafiaboy." These attacks targeted some of the most prominent websites on the internet, including Yahoo!, eBay, Amazon, CNN, and Dell, among others. Mafiaboy, whose real name is Michael Calce, executed a series of Distributed Denial of Service (DDoS) attacks that temporarily crippled these major websites, causing millions of dollars in losses and sparking widespread concern about internet security. This incident not only highlighted the vulnerabilities of even the most secure online platforms but also marked a pivotal moment in the history of cybersecurity.

The attacks began on February 7, 2000, with Yahoo!, one of the most visited websites at the time, being the first target. The DDoS attack overwhelmed Yahoo!'s servers with a flood of requests, causing the site to crash and remain offline for approximately three hours. This disruption was significant, given Yahoo!'s status as a leading internet portal and search engine. Following this initial attack, Mafiaboy launched similar assaults on other high-profile websites over the next week. Each attack involved bombarding the targeted site's servers with a massive volume of traffic, generated by networks of compromised computers, or "botnets," which effectively rendered the sites inaccessible to legitimate users.

The scale and audacity of these attacks drew immediate attention from the media, businesses, and government agencies. The fact that a single individual could disrupt major online services so profoundly exposed the fragility of the internet infrastructure and the potential for significant economic impact. Estimates of the financial damage caused by the attacks varied, but they were generally believed to run into tens of millions of dollars, factoring in lost revenue, remediation costs, and reputational damage to the affected companies.

The U.S. Federal Bureau of Investigation (FBI) and Canadian law enforcement agencies quickly launched investigations into the source of the attacks. The complexity of tracing the origins of DDoS attacks posed significant challenges, but investigators eventually traced the malicious traffic back to a network of compromised computers controlled by Mafiaboy. In April 2000, law enforcement officials arrested Michael Calce, a 15-year-old high school student from Montreal, Canada. The revelation that such a young individual was responsible for the attacks astonished the public and highlighted the accessibility of hacking tools and techniques.

Michael Calce's motivations for the attacks were not rooted in financial gain or political activism but rather in the desire to demonstrate his technical prowess and gain notoriety within the hacker community. During his trial, it was revealed that Calce had used relatively simple tools and scripts, readily available online, to orchestrate the attacks. This underscored the potential for even novice hackers to cause significant disruption using easily accessible resources, a sobering realization for cybersecurity experts and policymakers.

In September 2001, Calce pleaded guilty to multiple charges related to the cyberattacks, including mischief to data and unauthorized use of computer systems. He was sentenced to eight months in a youth detention center, one year of probation, and was prohibited from accessing the internet for a certain period. The relatively lenient sentence, attributed to his age and status as a first-time offender, sparked debate about the adequacy of legal frameworks to address cybercrime and the appropriate balance between punishment and rehabilitation for young offenders.

The Mafiaboy attacks had far-reaching implications for the field of cybersecurity. They served as a wake-up call for businesses, governments, and individuals about the vulnerabilities of online systems and the potential for widespread disruption caused by cyberattacks. In response to the attacks, many organizations began to reassess and strengthen their security measures, investing in more robust firewalls, intrusion detection systems, and other protective technologies. The incident also highlighted the need for better coordination and information sharing between private sector companies and government agencies to address and mitigate cyber threats.

On a broader scale, the Mafiaboy attacks contributed to the growing recognition of cybersecurity as a critical issue for national and economic security. Governments around the world began to take more proactive steps to enhance their cybersecurity capabilities, including the development of national strategies, the establishment of dedicated cybersecurity agencies, and the enactment of new laws and regulations aimed at deterring cybercrime and protecting critical infrastructure. In the United States, the attacks led to increased funding and support for initiatives like the National Infrastructure Protection Center and the National Cybersecurity Division, aimed at improving the country's ability to prevent and respond to cyber threats.

The incident also had a lasting impact on the hacker community and the broader culture of hacking. It highlighted the fine line between hacking for curiosity or fame and engaging in criminal activity with serious legal consequences. For many young hackers, the case of Mafiaboy served as a cautionary tale about the potential repercussions of their actions, prompting some to redirect their skills toward more positive and legitimate pursuits, such as ethical hacking and cybersecurity research.

Michael Calce's story did not end with his legal troubles. In the years following his arrest and conviction, he sought to use his experiences to raise awareness about cybersecurity issues and advocate for better security practices. He authored a book, "Mafiaboy: How I Cracked the Internet and Why It's Still Broken," in which he detailed his hacking exploits and offered insights into the vulnerabilities that persist in online systems. Calce also became a public speaker and security consultant, working to educate businesses and individuals about the importance of cybersecurity and the steps they can take to protect themselves from cyber threats.

The legacy of the Mafiaboy attacks continues to resonate in the field of cybersecurity. The incident underscored the evolving nature of cyber threats and the ongoing challenges in securing the internet against increasingly sophisticated and pervasive attacks. As the digital landscape has continued to grow and become more complex, the lessons learned from the Mafiaboy attacks remain relevant, emphasizing the need for vigilance, continuous improvement, and collaboration in the fight against cybercrime.

Chapter 4: Operation Shady RAT

Operation Shady RAT, an extensive and prolonged cyber espionage campaign discovered in 2011, stands as one of the most significant examples of state-sponsored hacking in the early 21st century. Conducted over a five-year period from 2006 to 2011, this operation targeted a diverse range of entities, including government agencies, international organizations, corporations, and non-profits across 14 countries. The operation's name, "Shady RAT" (Remote Access Tool), was coined by McAfee, the cybersecurity firm that uncovered and analyzed the campaign. The revelation of this sophisticated and persistent cyber espionage effort highlighted the vulnerabilities of global digital infrastructure and underscored the evolving threat of state-sponsored cyber operations.

The origins of Operation Shady RAT can be traced back to mid-2006 when the first known infiltrations occurred. However, it wasn't until 2011 that the full scope of the operation came to light. McAfee discovered the campaign while investigating suspicious network activity across its clients. Through extensive forensic analysis, McAfee researchers identified a coordinated and systematic effort to compromise and extract sensitive data from a wide array of targets. The targets included government departments, defense contractors, multinational corporations, non-governmental organizations (NGOs), and international sporting bodies, notably those associated with the Olympics.

The method employed by the attackers was relatively straightforward yet highly effective. They used spear-phishing emails to deliver malicious payloads to specific individuals within the targeted organizations. These emails, crafted to appear legitimate and often personalized to increase the likelihood of being opened, contained attachments or links that, when executed, installed a remote access tool (RAT) on the victim's computer. Once the RAT was in place, it allowed the attackers to gain complete control over the infected system, enabling them to move laterally across networks, escalate privileges, and exfiltrate sensitive data.

One of the notable aspects of Operation Shady RAT was its persistence and the longevity of the infections. In many cases, the attackers maintained access to compromised networks for several years without detection. This persistence was facilitated by the stealthy nature of the malware used and the attackers' ability to continuously update and modify their tools to evade detection by antivirus software and intrusion detection systems. The exfiltrated data included a wide range of sensitive information, such as intellectual property, proprietary business information, strategic plans, and classified government documents.

The discovery of Operation Shady RAT sent shockwaves through the cybersecurity community and beyond. The sheer scale and duration of the campaign underscored the vulnerabilities of even the most security-conscious organizations. It also highlighted the limitations of existing security measures and the need for more robust and adaptive defenses. The operation's exposure led to widespread concern about the state of global cybersecurity and the potential for similar attacks in the future.

The geopolitical implications of Operation Shady RAT were significant. Although McAfee did not publicly attribute the attacks to any specific nation, the nature of the targets and the sophistication of the operation suggested state-sponsored involvement. Many experts and analysts pointed to China as the likely origin of the attacks, citing the strategic interests reflected in the choice of targets and the pattern of activity consistent with other known Chinese cyber espionage efforts. This attribution, while not officially confirmed, fueled ongoing debates about state-sponsored cyber activities and the rules of engagement in cyberspace.

The response to the revelation of Operation Shady RAT varied across different sectors and regions. Governments and private sector organizations alike took steps to reassess their cybersecurity postures and implement more stringent security measures. This included enhancing network monitoring capabilities, improving incident response protocols, and increasing investments in cybersecurity technologies and personnel. Additionally, the operation underscored the importance of information sharing and collaboration between public and private entities to effectively combat sophisticated cyber threats.

The long-term impact of Operation Shady RAT on the field of cybersecurity was profound. It served as a catalyst for significant advancements in threat detection and response capabilities. The operation highlighted the need for continuous monitoring and analysis of network activity to detect and respond to advanced persistent threats (APTs). It also underscored the importance of developing more sophisticated and automated threat intelligence systems to identify and mitigate emerging threats in real time.

In the aftermath of Operation Shady RAT, there was a growing recognition of the importance of cybersecurity as a critical component of national security and economic stability. Governments around the world began to take more proactive steps to enhance their cybersecurity capabilities, including the establishment of national cybersecurity centers, the development of comprehensive cybersecurity strategies, and the enactment of new laws and regulations aimed at protecting critical infrastructure and sensitive information from cyber threats. These efforts were complemented by increased international cooperation and the establishment of norms and frameworks to govern state behavior in cyberspace.

The private sector also responded to the lessons learned from Operation Shady RAT by adopting more rigorous security practices and investing in advanced security technologies. Companies recognized the importance of a multi-layered defense strategy that included not only traditional perimeter defenses but also advanced threat detection and response capabilities, endpoint protection, and user awareness training. The operation also highlighted the need for a more proactive approach to cybersecurity, with organizations increasingly focusing on threat hunting and red teaming exercises to identify and address potential vulnerabilities before they could be exploited by attackers.

Operation Shady RAT also had a lasting impact on the broader discourse around cybersecurity and privacy. The operation underscored the pervasive nature of cyber espionage and the potential for state-sponsored actors to conduct long-term and wide-ranging surveillance and data exfiltration activities. This raised important questions about the balance between national security and individual privacy, the role of governments in protecting citizens' digital rights, and the ethical implications of state-sponsored cyber activities.

Chapter 5: TJX Data Breach

The TJX data breach of 2007 remains one of the most significant and impactful cybercrimes in history. The breach was discovered by the company in mid-December 2006 but is believed to have begun as early as July 2005. TJX Companies Inc., a major retailer operating brands such as T.J. Maxx, Marshalls, HomeGoods, and others, was the victim of this massive security breach that exposed the personal and financial information of over 45 million credit and debit card holders, though some estimates suggest the number could be as high as 94 million.

The breach occurred due to weaknesses in the company's network security. Hackers exploited several vulnerabilities, including outdated encryption standards and poor network configuration, to infiltrate TJX's systems. The primary method used by the attackers involved a technique called war driving, which entails searching for unsecured wireless networks while traveling in a vehicle. The hackers were able to gain access to TJX's network by intercepting data from poorly protected wireless access points in two stores in Miami, Florida.

Once inside the network, the attackers utilized a variety of methods to capture and extract data. They deployed malware to harvest payment card information from the transaction processing system, targeting unencrypted data that was momentarily visible during the processing of transactions. Additionally, the attackers took advantage of weak password policies and insufficiently protected access points to move laterally within the network, accessing central databases that stored customer information.

The data extracted included credit and debit card numbers, names, addresses, and other sensitive information. The stolen data was then sold on the black market or used directly by the hackers for fraudulent purchases. The breach had significant financial repercussions for TJX, with the company facing hundreds of millions of dollars in costs related to the breach, including settlements with affected customers, banks, and credit card companies, as well as expenses for legal fees and security upgrades.

The fallout from the breach extended beyond financial losses for TJX. The company suffered reputational damage, leading to a loss of consumer trust and a decline in stock value. Furthermore, the incident highlighted the need for stronger security measures within the retail industry and served as a wake-up call for other companies to reassess their cybersecurity practices.

In the aftermath of the breach, TJX took several steps to improve its security posture. The company upgraded its encryption standards, implemented stronger access controls, and enhanced its monitoring and detection capabilities to better protect against future attacks. Despite these efforts, the TJX data breach remains a cautionary tale about the importance of robust cybersecurity measures and the potential consequences of failing to adequately protect sensitive customer information.

The legal consequences for those involved in the breach were significant. Several individuals were arrested and prosecuted for their roles in the attack. Notably, Albert Gonzalez, a prominent figure in the hacking community, was identified as a key orchestrator of the breach. Gonzalez, who had previously cooperated with law enforcement as an informant, was found to have masterminded a series of high-profile data breaches, including the TJX incident. He was ultimately sentenced to 20 years in prison for his involvement in these crimes, one of the longest sentences ever handed down for a cybercrime at the time.

The TJX data breach also prompted regulatory and legislative responses aimed at strengthening data security requirements for businesses. The Payment Card Industry Data Security Standard (PCI DSS) was updated to address some of the vulnerabilities exploited in the TJX breach, emphasizing the need for encryption, secure wireless networks, and comprehensive monitoring of network activity. Additionally, several states enacted data breach notification laws, requiring companies to promptly inform affected individuals and authorities when a data breach occurs.

Overall, the TJX data breach serves as a landmark case in the history of cybercrime. It underscores the importance of proactive cybersecurity measures, the evolving nature of cyber threats, and the far-reaching impacts of data breaches on companies, consumers, and the broader economy. The lessons learned from the TJX incident continue to influence how organizations approach data security, highlighting the necessity for continuous vigilance, investment in advanced security technologies, and a commitment to protecting sensitive information in an increasingly digital world.

Chapter 6: Conficker Worm

The Conficker worm, also known as Downup, Downadup, or Kido, is one of the most infamous and widespread pieces of malware in the history of cybersecurity. First detected in November 2008, Conficker exploited a vulnerability in the Windows operating system to spread rapidly across networks, creating one of the largest botnets ever seen. The worm is notorious not only for its technical sophistication but also for its enduring presence and the substantial impact it had on millions of computers worldwide.

Conficker spread by exploiting the MS08-067 vulnerability, a flaw in the Windows Server service that allowed remote code execution. Microsoft had released a patch for this vulnerability in October 2008, but many systems remained unpatched, providing fertile ground for the worm's propagation. Once a system was infected, Conficker used a variety of techniques to ensure its persistence and spread to other vulnerable machines. These techniques included exploiting weak passwords, leveraging removable media such as USB drives, and employing sophisticated methods to evade detection and removal.

One of the key features of Conficker was its use of a sophisticated algorithm to generate domain names for command and control (C&C) servers. This algorithm created hundreds of new domain names each day, making it extremely difficult for security researchers and law enforcement to track and shut down the worm's communication channels. Additionally, Conficker was designed to disable security services, block access to security websites, and prevent the installation of security updates, further complicating efforts to eradicate the infection.

The worm's impact was significant, affecting millions of computers in both the private and public sectors. In January 2009, an estimated 15 million systems were infected, making it one of the largest known botnets at the time. Conficker caused substantial disruptions in various organizations, including military and government agencies, businesses, and educational institutions. The worm's ability to disable security measures and spread rapidly through networks meant that it could cripple entire IT infrastructures, leading to operational and financial losses.

One notable example of Conficker's impact was its infiltration of the French Navy's computer systems in early 2009. The infection forced the Navy to ground its fleet of Rafale fighter jets temporarily, as the malware disrupted the systems used for flight operations. Similarly, the United Kingdom's Ministry of Defence reported infections on approximately 24 critical systems, highlighting the worm's ability to penetrate high-security environments. Numerous hospitals, police departments, and universities also fell victim to Conficker, demonstrating its wide-reaching consequences.

The cybersecurity community mobilized quickly to combat the Conficker worm. The Conficker Working Group (CWG), a coalition of security researchers, industry experts, and law enforcement agencies, was formed to coordinate efforts to mitigate the threat. The CWG focused on several key areas, including identifying and neutralizing the C&C servers, developing tools to detect and remove the infection, and raising awareness about the importance of patching vulnerabilities and maintaining robust security practices.

One of the CWG's significant achievements was the takedown of several C&C domains generated by the worm's algorithm. By registering these domains preemptively, the group was able to disrupt Conficker's ability to communicate with its controllers, effectively hampering its operations. Additionally, the CWG released a series of detection and removal tools that helped organizations identify and clean infected systems. Despite these efforts, Conficker's sophisticated design and ability to evolve meant that it continued to pose a threat for several years.

The long-term impact of the Conficker worm extends beyond the immediate damage it caused. The incident highlighted critical weaknesses in the cybersecurity practices of many organizations, particularly the importance of timely patching and robust password policies. Conficker also underscored the need for greater international collaboration in combating cyber threats, as the worm's spread across borders demonstrated the global nature of such threats.

In response to Conficker, Microsoft implemented several measures to improve security and prevent similar incidents in the future. These measures included enhancing the Windows Update service to ensure more reliable and timely delivery of security patches, improving the default security settings in Windows, and promoting better awareness and education about cybersecurity best practices among users and administrators.

The Conficker worm also had a lasting impact on the cybersecurity landscape, driving advancements in malware detection and response techniques. Researchers and security companies developed new methods for analyzing and countering sophisticated malware, including better heuristic analysis, machine learning algorithms, and collaborative threat intelligence sharing. These advancements have contributed to the development of more resilient defenses against future cyber threats.

Chapter 7: Operation Aurora

Operation Aurora, discovered in late 2009 and publicly disclosed by Google in January 2010, stands as one of the most notable and sophisticated cyber-espionage campaigns of its time. The operation was a highly targeted attack that infiltrated the computer systems of over 20 major companies, including Google, Adobe Systems, Juniper Networks, and more. This cyber-attack is widely believed to have originated in China, though definitive attribution remains a subject of debate and speculation.

The attack utilized a zero-day vulnerability in Internet Explorer, which was exploited to gain a foothold within the targeted networks. This vulnerability allowed attackers to execute remote code on the compromised systems. The initial point of entry was typically through spear-phishing emails sent to specific individuals within the organizations. These emails contained links to malicious websites that hosted the exploit code. Once the exploit was successfully executed, a backdoor known as Hydraq was installed, providing the attackers with persistent access to the infected systems.

One of the primary objectives of Operation Aurora appeared to be the theft of intellectual property and sensitive corporate data. In Google's case, the attackers sought access to Gmail accounts of Chinese human rights activists, marking a notable instance of cyber-espionage with political motivations. The attackers were able to infiltrate Google's corporate network, accessing a repository containing proprietary source code and sensitive information related to Google's operations. This breach prompted Google to reconsider its business operations in China, ultimately leading to a significant reduction in its presence in the country.

The sophistication of Operation Aurora was evident in the methods used to cover the attackers' tracks and maintain persistence within the compromised networks. The malware employed advanced techniques to avoid detection, including the use of encrypted communications and the ability to download additional payloads as needed. The attackers also used legitimate administrative credentials obtained through social engineering and other means, enabling them to move laterally within the networks and escalate their privileges.

The disclosure of Operation Aurora had far-reaching implications for the cybersecurity community and the companies involved. For Google, the attack was a catalyst for a broader reassessment of its security posture and policies. The company took significant steps to enhance its security infrastructure, including the implementation of more robust encryption for data in transit and at rest, the adoption of multi-factor authentication for employees, and the establishment of a dedicated threat analysis group to monitor and respond to future threats.

The attack also highlighted the importance of collaboration and information sharing among companies and government agencies in combating sophisticated cyber threats. In the wake of the disclosure, affected companies and cybersecurity experts worked together to analyze the attack, identify the techniques used, and develop countermeasures. This collaboration led to the creation of indicators of compromise (IOCs) and the dissemination of information that helped other organizations protect themselves against similar threats.

Operation Aurora underscored the evolving nature of cyber threats and the increasing sophistication of state-sponsored attacks. The incident demonstrated that traditional security measures, such as firewalls and antivirus software, were insufficient to protect against advanced persistent threats (APTs). This realization spurred the development and adoption of more advanced security technologies, including behavioral analysis, threat intelligence platforms, and endpoint detection and response (EDR) solutions.

Moreover, the attack had a lasting impact on cybersecurity policies and practices at the national and international levels. Governments around the world took note of the incident, recognizing the need for stronger cybersecurity defenses and greater investment in cyber capabilities. The U.S. government, in particular, ramped up its efforts to enhance national cybersecurity, including the establishment of the Cyber Threat Intelligence Integration Center (CTIIC) to coordinate and analyze cyber threat information across different agencies.

For the companies affected, the financial and reputational consequences of Operation Aurora were significant. The direct costs associated with incident response, remediation, and legal fees were substantial. Additionally, the loss of intellectual property and sensitive data had long-term implications for competitive advantage and market position. Companies also faced increased scrutiny from regulators, customers, and shareholders, leading to a greater emphasis on transparency and accountability in cybersecurity practices.

The lessons learned from Operation Aurora continue to resonate within the cybersecurity community. The incident highlighted the critical importance of proactive threat hunting, continuous monitoring, and rapid incident response capabilities. Organizations have since adopted more comprehensive security frameworks, such as the NIST Cybersecurity Framework and the MITRE ATT&CK framework, to guide their defenses against sophisticated threats. These frameworks emphasize a holistic approach to cybersecurity, encompassing not only technical controls but also governance, risk management, and workforce training.

Chapter 8: Stuxnet

Stuxnet, discovered in 2010, is widely regarded as one of the most sophisticated and groundbreaking pieces of malware ever created. It marked a significant milestone in cyber warfare, as it was the first known cyber weapon specifically designed to target industrial control systems (ICS). The malware is believed to have been jointly developed by the United States and Israel to sabotage Iran's nuclear enrichment capabilities. Its primary target was the centrifuges at the Natanz uranium enrichment facility, which were essential for Iran's nuclear program.

The complexity and sophistication of Stuxnet set it apart from previous cyber threats. Unlike conventional malware, which often aims to steal data or cause general disruption, Stuxnet was engineered to achieve a specific physical effect: the sabotage of industrial machinery. It did this by exploiting multiple zero-day vulnerabilities in Microsoft Windows and Siemens software, allowing it to spread undetected and manipulate the operations of the targeted industrial equipment.

Stuxnet's attack vector involved infecting Windows-based computers via infected USB flash drives. Once a system was compromised, the worm sought out Siemens Step7 software, which is used to program industrial control systems. The malware then modified the PLC (Programmable Logic Controller) code without alerting the operators, causing the centrifuges to spin at unsafe speeds while simultaneously providing normal readings to monitoring systems. This dual action resulted in the physical degradation and eventual destruction of the centrifuges while keeping the sabotage hidden from the plant operators.

The design of Stuxnet included several innovative features. First, it utilized four zero-day exploits, which are vulnerabilities unknown to the software vendor and without available patches. This made Stuxnet exceptionally potent and difficult to detect. Second, it had a sophisticated command and control structure that allowed it to receive updates and instructions from remote servers. Third, the malware included a self-replication mechanism that allowed it to spread across networks, infecting other machines while remaining stealthy.

One of the most remarkable aspects of Stuxnet was its ability to remain dormant and undetected for extended periods. It contained advanced evasion techniques, such as rootkits, which concealed its presence from antivirus software and other security measures. The worm was designed to activate only under specific conditions, ensuring it targeted only the intended systems and minimizing collateral damage.

The discovery of Stuxnet was a watershed moment for cybersecurity experts. It was first identified by a Belarusian security firm, VirusBlokAda, which found the worm on a client's computer in June 2010. Further analysis by Symantec and other cybersecurity firms revealed the true extent and purpose of the malware. Researchers were astounded by its complexity, and its discovery led to widespread media coverage and a reevaluation of the potential for cyber weapons to cause real-world damage.

The impact of Stuxnet on Iran's nuclear program was significant. Reports indicate that the malware destroyed around 1,000 of the 5,000 centrifuges at the Natanz facility, setting back Iran's nuclear enrichment efforts by several years. The attack demonstrated the potential for cyber operations to achieve strategic objectives without conventional military intervention.

Stuxnet also had far-reaching implications for global cybersecurity and industrial control systems. It highlighted the vulnerabilities of critical infrastructure to cyber-attacks and underscored the need for improved security measures. In the wake of Stuxnet, governments and organizations worldwide intensified their focus on securing industrial control systems and critical infrastructure. This included the development of new cybersecurity standards, increased investment in defensive technologies, and greater collaboration between the public and private sectors.

The revelation of Stuxnet's origins and purpose sparked significant debate about the ethics and legality of using cyber weapons. It raised questions about the norms of state behavior in cyberspace and the potential for escalation and unintended consequences. The attack demonstrated that nation-states could leverage cyber capabilities to achieve strategic objectives, but it also highlighted the potential for collateral damage and the risk of such tools falling into the hands of non-state actors or being repurposed for other malicious activities.

Stuxnet's legacy continues to influence cybersecurity practices and policies. It served as a wake-up call for industries that rely on ICS, prompting them to reassess their security postures and adopt more robust protective measures. Organizations have since implemented stronger network segmentation, regular patching of software vulnerabilities, enhanced monitoring, and incident response capabilities to detect and mitigate similar threats.

Furthermore, Stuxnet's impact extended to the development of cybersecurity frameworks and regulations. The incident prompted the establishment of new guidelines and standards for protecting critical infrastructure, such as the National Institute of Standards and Technology (NIST) Cybersecurity Framework and the European Union's Network and Information Systems (NIS) Directive. These frameworks provide organizations with a structured approach to managing cybersecurity risks and improving their resilience against advanced threats.

In addition to its technical and operational significance, Stuxnet also left a lasting imprint on the discourse surrounding cyber warfare and national security. It demonstrated the potential for cyber operations to achieve strategic objectives traditionally reserved for kinetic military action, reshaping the strategic landscape and prompting nations to invest in offensive and defensive cyber capabilities. The incident underscored the need for international norms and agreements to govern state behavior in cyberspace, aiming to prevent the proliferation of cyber weapons and reduce the risk of conflict escalation.

Chapter 9: Operation Payback

Operation Payback, a series of high-profile cyber-attacks orchestrated by the hacktivist group Anonymous in 2010, stands as a landmark event in the history of digital activism and cyber warfare. The campaign was initially launched as a response to actions taken by organizations against online piracy, but it soon expanded to target a variety of entities perceived by Anonymous to be antagonistic to internet freedom. The operation underscored the growing power and influence of decentralized hacker collectives in shaping digital and political landscapes.

The genesis of Operation Payback can be traced back to September 2010, when several major copyright protection organizations, such as the Motion Picture Association of America (MPAA) and the Recording Industry Association of America (RIAA), initiated legal actions and other measures to shut down file-sharing websites like The Pirate Bay and targeting platforms like LimeWire. These actions were viewed by Anonymous as attempts to censor the internet and restrict access to information. In retaliation, Anonymous launched a series of Distributed Denial of Service (DDoS) attacks against the websites of these organizations, effectively taking them offline and disrupting their operations.

DDoS attacks, the primary weapon in Anonymous's arsenal during Operation Payback, involve overwhelming a target website with a massive influx of traffic, rendering it inaccessible to legitimate users. Anonymous utilized a tool known as the Low Orbit Ion Cannon (LOIC), which allowed participants to voluntarily contribute their computing power to the attack. This method of crowd-sourced hacking democratized cyber activism, enabling individuals worldwide to join the cause with minimal technical expertise.

As the campaign progressed, Operation Payback's scope widened to encompass a broader array of targets, reflecting Anonymous's evolving agenda. The group's focus shifted to include entities involved in what it perceived as broader abuses of power and infringements on internet freedom. This included attacks on law firms involved in anti-piracy litigation, such as ACS (Andrew Crossley Solicitors), which had been sending threatening letters to alleged file-sharers demanding monetary settlements. When Anonymous targeted ACS, the firm's website was not only taken offline, but a misconfiguration during its recovery attempt led to the exposure of sensitive emails and documents, causing significant embarrassment and legal repercussions for the firm.

In December 2010, Operation Payback took a dramatic turn with the advent of the WikiLeaks controversy. WikiLeaks, the whistleblower organization, had released a vast trove of classified U.S. diplomatic cables, leading to intense governmental and corporate backlash. When major financial institutions like PayPal, Visa, and MasterCard, as well as companies like Amazon, withdrew their services from WikiLeaks under government pressure, Anonymous perceived these actions as attempts to stifle free speech and transparency. In response, Anonymous launched a new phase of Operation Payback, which it dubbed "Operation Avenge Assange," named after WikiLeaks founder Julian Assange.

The attacks on PayPal, Visa, and MasterCard were particularly impactful, highlighting Anonymous's ability to disrupt major financial services. The DDoS attacks temporarily crippled the websites of these companies, drawing significant media attention and sparking debates about the balance between corporate compliance with government directives and the principles of free speech and transparency. The attacks also garnered widespread public support for Anonymous, with many individuals viewing the campaign as a defense of internet freedom and a stand against corporate and governmental overreach.

Operation Payback's impact extended beyond the immediate disruption of targeted websites. The campaign brought significant attention to the issues of digital rights, internet censorship, and the power dynamics between corporations, governments, and the public. It also demonstrated the potential for decentralized, leaderless movements to mobilize large numbers of individuals for coordinated cyber actions. Anonymous's use of social media and online forums to organize and communicate with supporters exemplified a new model of digital activism that could rapidly respond to perceived injustices.

The legal and political ramifications of Operation Payback were substantial. Governments and law enforcement agencies around the world took notice of the growing threat posed by Anonymous and similar hacker collectives. Efforts to identify and prosecute individuals involved in the attacks intensified, leading to a number of arrests and legal actions against suspected members of Anonymous. These prosecutions highlighted the challenges of attributing cyber-attacks to specific individuals within a decentralized and anonymous collective, as well as the difficulties in balancing security with civil liberties.

Operation Payback also influenced the cybersecurity landscape, prompting organizations to reevaluate their defenses against DDoS attacks and other forms of cyber aggression. Companies targeted by Anonymous were forced to invest in more robust security measures and incident response capabilities, while other organizations took preemptive steps to protect themselves against potential future attacks. The campaign underscored the need for improved cybersecurity practices and heightened awareness of the evolving threat landscape.

The legacy of Operation Payback continues to resonate within the realms of digital activism and cybersecurity. The campaign is often cited as a key example of the power of collective action in the digital age, demonstrating how decentralized networks can leverage technology to challenge powerful entities and advocate for social and political change. It also serves as a cautionary tale about the potential for cyber-attacks to disrupt critical infrastructure and services, highlighting the ongoing need for vigilance and resilience in the face of emerging threats.

Chapter 10: Sony PlayStation Network Hack

The Sony PlayStation Network (PSN) hack of 2011 stands as one of the most significant and impactful data breaches in the history of cybersecurity. The breach, which occurred in April 2011, led to the exposure of personal information belonging to approximately 77 million accounts, marking it as one of the largest data breaches involving a gaming network. The incident not only highlighted critical vulnerabilities in Sony's network security but also had profound repercussions for the company, its users, and the broader gaming and cybersecurity communities.

The attack began on April 17, 2011, when malicious actors infiltrated Sony's PlayStation Network. The intrusion was not discovered until April 19, and Sony promptly shut down the network on April 20 to prevent further damage and begin an investigation. During this period, attackers were able to access and exfiltrate a vast amount of data, including users' names, addresses, email addresses, birthdates, and login credentials. Additionally, it was suspected that credit card information might have been compromised, although Sony later stated that there was no evidence that encrypted credit card data had been accessed.

The immediate impact of the breach was severe. The PlayStation Network was taken offline for 23 days, during which time users were unable to access online gaming services, download games and updates, or use other network-related features. This outage led to widespread frustration and anger among PlayStation users, many of whom took to social media and forums to express their dissatisfaction. The incident also disrupted the operations of developers and publishers who relied on the network to distribute their games and content.

Sony's handling of the breach came under intense scrutiny. The company faced criticism for the delay in informing users about the extent of the breach and the potential risks to their personal information. It was not until April 26, a week after the network was taken offline, that Sony publicly disclosed the full scope of the data breach. This delay in communication exacerbated the backlash from users and raised questions about Sony's transparency and crisis management practices.

In response to the breach, Sony undertook a comprehensive review and overhaul of its network security measures. The company hired external security firms to conduct a thorough investigation of the breach and identify the vulnerabilities that had been exploited. Sony implemented a series of significant security enhancements, including the addition of advanced encryption methods, enhanced firewalls, and more robust intrusion detection systems. Additionally, Sony moved its data center to a new, more secure location and introduced a new software monitoring system designed to detect and respond to security threats more effectively.

To compensate users for the disruption and potential loss of personal data, Sony offered a "Welcome Back" program, which included free games, a month of free PlayStation Plus membership, and complimentary identity theft protection services. This initiative aimed to restore user trust and loyalty, although the damage to Sony's reputation was considerable and took time to repair.

The legal and financial ramifications of the breach were substantial. Sony faced numerous lawsuits from users and financial institutions, alleging negligence and seeking compensation for damages. In addition, the company was subjected to investigations by various government agencies, including the U.S. Congress, the U.K. Information Commissioner's Office, and data protection authorities in other countries. These investigations led to calls for stronger data protection regulations and more stringent oversight of companies handling large volumes of personal information.

The financial impact of the breach on Sony was significant. The company estimated that the total cost of the incident, including legal fees, settlements, and the expenses associated with network security improvements and user compensation, was around $171 million. This figure does not account for the longer-term effects on Sony's brand and customer trust, which were more difficult to quantify but undoubtedly profound.

The PlayStation Network hack of 2011 also had broader implications for the cybersecurity and gaming industries. It served as a stark reminder of the vulnerabilities inherent in online networks and the potential consequences of inadequate security measures. The incident prompted other companies in the gaming industry to reassess their own security practices and invest in more robust defenses against cyber threats. It also heightened awareness among consumers about the importance of data security and the risks associated with sharing personal information online.

In the aftermath of the breach, the cybersecurity landscape saw increased emphasis on proactive threat detection and response strategies. Companies began to adopt more advanced technologies, such as artificial intelligence and machine learning, to identify and mitigate potential threats before they could cause significant damage. Additionally, there was a greater focus on incident response planning and the development of comprehensive crisis management protocols to ensure timely and effective action in the event of a breach.

The Sony PlayStation Network hack also influenced regulatory developments in data protection. The breach underscored the need for stronger data privacy laws and more rigorous enforcement of existing regulations. In the years following the incident, there was a push for enhanced data protection frameworks, such as the European Union's General Data Protection Regulation (GDPR), which introduced stricter requirements for data handling and breach notification, as well as significant penalties for non-compliance.

Moreover, the breach highlighted the importance of user education and awareness in cybersecurity. Consumers became more cognizant of the risks associated with online activities and the need to take proactive steps to protect their personal information. This included practices such as using strong, unique passwords for different accounts, enabling two-factor authentication, and being vigilant about phishing attempts and other social engineering attacks.

The Sony PlayStation Network hack of 2011 remains a pivotal event in the history of cybersecurity. It demonstrated the potentially devastating consequences of cyber-attacks on large-scale networks and the critical importance of robust security measures. The incident served as a catalyst for significant changes in the way companies approach cybersecurity, influencing industry practices, regulatory frameworks, and consumer awareness. While the immediate aftermath of the breach was marked by significant challenges for Sony, the lessons learned from the incident have contributed to a more secure and resilient digital environment.

Chapter 11: Yahoo! Data Breaches

The Yahoo! data breaches of 2013 and 2014 represent some of the largest and most devastating cyberattacks in history, significantly impacting millions of users and the company itself. The breaches, which were only disclosed to the public in 2016, involved the theft of data from all of Yahoo's user accounts, approximately 3 billion in total, and had profound implications for the fields of cybersecurity, corporate responsibility, and regulatory policy.

The first breach, which occurred in August 2013, compromised the personal information of all 3 billion Yahoo! user accounts. This included names, email addresses, telephone numbers, dates of birth, hashed passwords (most using the outdated MD5 hashing algorithm), and, in some cases, encrypted or unencrypted security questions and answers. The attackers exploited a vulnerability in Yahoo's system to gain unauthorized access and extract this massive trove of data. Despite the breach's severity, it went undetected by Yahoo! for years.

The second major breach occurred in late 2014 and was discovered by Yahoo! in late 2016. This attack compromised an additional 500 million user accounts. The stolen information was similar to that taken in the 2013 breach and included names, email addresses, telephone numbers, dates of birth, hashed passwords, and security questions and answers. Yahoo! attributed the 2014 breach to a state-sponsored actor, although specifics about the attackers were not disclosed.

Yahoo! initially reported the 2014 breach in September 2016, describing it as one of the largest data breaches ever recorded at that time. However, it wasn't until October 2017 that Yahoo! revealed the full extent of the 2013 breach, admitting that all 3 billion accounts had been compromised. This staggered disclosure raised significant concerns about Yahoo's security practices and transparency, as the company had failed to identify and communicate the breaches promptly.

The delayed and incomplete disclosure had substantial repercussions for Yahoo!. The breaches occurred during a period when Yahoo! was negotiating its sale to Verizon Communications. Originally, the deal was valued at $4.8 billion, but the discovery of the breaches led to a renegotiation of the sale price, resulting in a $350 million reduction. The financial impact was considerable, and the reputational damage to Yahoo! was immense, undermining user trust and confidence in the company's ability to protect personal information.

The technical aspects of the breaches highlighted several critical security failures within Yahoo!'s infrastructure. The use of outdated and weak encryption methods, such as MD5 hashing for passwords, made it easier for attackers to decrypt and exploit the stolen data. Additionally, Yahoo!'s security measures were inadequate in detecting and responding to the breaches in a timely manner. The lack of multi-factor authentication and other modern security practices further exacerbated the vulnerabilities.

The Yahoo! breaches also underscored the challenges organizations face in managing cybersecurity threats and protecting sensitive data. Despite being a major internet company, Yahoo! failed to implement robust security protocols and monitoring systems, which allowed the breaches to go undetected for extended periods. This highlighted the need for continuous investment in cybersecurity infrastructure and the importance of staying updated with the latest security practices and technologies.

The fallout from the Yahoo! breaches had broader implications for the cybersecurity industry and regulatory landscape. The incident served as a stark reminder of the potential consequences of data breaches, prompting companies across various sectors to reevaluate their security measures and prioritize the protection of user data. The breaches also influenced the development and enforcement of stricter data protection regulations globally.

In the United States, the Yahoo! breaches contributed to increased scrutiny by regulatory bodies such as the Securities and Exchange Commission (SEC) and the Federal Trade Commission (FTC). In April 2018, the SEC fined Yahoo! $35 million for failing to disclose the breaches to investors in a timely manner. The FTC also reached a settlement with Yahoo! in April 2019, requiring the company to implement a comprehensive data security program and undergo regular third-party assessments for 20 years.

The breaches had a significant impact on individual users, many of whom experienced the fallout of having their personal information exposed. The compromised data could be used in various malicious activities, including identity theft, phishing attacks, and other forms of cybercrime. The breaches underscored the importance of personal cybersecurity practices, such as using strong, unique passwords for different accounts, enabling multi-factor authentication, and regularly monitoring accounts for suspicious activity.

In addition to regulatory and user impacts, the breaches influenced corporate governance and accountability. Yahoo!'s senior management, including CEO Marissa Mayer, faced criticism for their handling of the incidents. Mayer ultimately lost her annual bonus and equity compensation, which was redistributed to Yahoo! employees. The breaches highlighted the need for executive accountability in cybersecurity matters and the importance of incorporating security into corporate governance frameworks.

The Yahoo! data breaches also played a role in the evolution of global data protection laws. The European Union's General Data Protection Regulation (GDPR), which came into effect in May 2018, introduced stringent requirements for data breach notification and imposed heavy fines for non-compliance. The Yahoo! breaches illustrated the necessity of such regulations, emphasizing the need for companies to protect personal data and promptly inform affected individuals and authorities in the event of a breach.

The aftermath of the Yahoo! breaches saw significant changes in how organizations approach cybersecurity. Companies increasingly adopted more advanced security technologies, such as encryption, intrusion detection systems, and behavioral analytics, to safeguard their networks and data. There was also a greater emphasis on cybersecurity training and awareness programs for employees, recognizing that human error often plays a critical role in security incidents.

Chapter 12: Target Data Breach

The Target data breach of 2013 is one of the most notorious and far-reaching cyberattacks in the history of retail cybersecurity. It resulted in the exposure of personal and financial information of tens of millions of customers and highlighted significant vulnerabilities in corporate security practices. The breach, which occurred during the busy holiday shopping season, had profound implications for Target, its customers, and the broader cybersecurity landscape.

The breach began in November 2013, when cybercriminals gained unauthorized access to Target's network. The attackers used a sophisticated method to infiltrate the system: they initially compromised a third-party vendor, Fazio Mechanical Services, which provided refrigeration and HVAC services to Target. The attackers obtained credentials from Fazio, which allowed them to access Target's network. This method of breaching a larger target by first compromising a smaller, less secure third-party vendor is known as a supply chain attack.

Once inside Target's network, the attackers installed malware on the company's point-of-sale (POS) systems. This malware, known as a RAM scraper, was designed to capture credit card data from the magnetic stripes of payment cards as they were swiped at cash registers. The stolen data included credit and debit card numbers, expiration dates, card verification values (CVVs), and other sensitive information.

The breach went undetected for several weeks, during which time the attackers managed to exfiltrate data on approximately 40 million credit and debit card accounts. Additionally, personal information, including names, addresses, phone numbers, and email addresses of around 70 million customers, was also compromised. The stolen data was subsequently transferred to servers controlled by the attackers, believed to be located in Eastern Europe.

The breach was discovered on December 15, 2013, when a major U.S. credit card issuer noticed a spike in fraudulent transactions. Target was informed of the suspicious activity and launched an internal investigation. On December 19, 2013, Target publicly acknowledged the breach, informing customers that their payment information had been compromised. This announcement came just days before Christmas, one of the busiest shopping periods of the year, adding to the chaos and concern among consumers.

The immediate aftermath of the breach was chaotic and costly for Target. The company faced a barrage of criticism for its handling of the incident, particularly regarding the delay in detecting the breach and notifying affected customers. Target's CEO at the time, Gregg Steinhafel, issued a public apology and the company offered free credit monitoring and identity theft protection to affected customers. Despite these efforts, the damage to Target's reputation was significant.

The financial impact of the breach on Target was substantial. The company incurred hundreds of millions of dollars in expenses related to the breach, including costs for customer notifications, credit monitoring services, legal fees, and settlements with banks and credit card companies. In addition, Target faced numerous lawsuits from customers and financial institutions, alleging negligence and seeking compensation for damages.

In 2015, Target agreed to pay $10 million to settle a class-action lawsuit filed by customers affected by the breach. Additionally, the company reached settlements with several state attorneys general, agreeing to pay millions of dollars in fines and to implement more robust security measures. The breach also led to significant changes in Target's leadership, with CEO Gregg Steinhafel resigning in May 2014 as a result of the fallout.

The Target data breach had broader implications for the retail and cybersecurity industries. It served as a wake-up call for companies about the importance of robust cybersecurity measures and the potential consequences of failing to protect customer data. The breach highlighted several key vulnerabilities, including the risks associated with third-party vendors, the need for advanced threat detection and response capabilities, and the importance of encrypting sensitive data.

In response to the breach, many retailers and other organizations began to reevaluate and strengthen their cybersecurity practices. This included implementing more rigorous security protocols, such as encrypting payment card data, using more advanced intrusion detection systems, and conducting regular security audits. The breach also accelerated the adoption of EMV (Europay, MasterCard, and Visa) chip technology in the United States, which provides more secure payment processing compared to traditional magnetic stripe cards.

The Target breach also influenced regulatory and legislative developments in cybersecurity. In the United States, the breach contributed to the push for stronger data protection laws and more stringent requirements for reporting data breaches. Several states enacted new laws mandating faster notification of data breaches and imposing stricter penalties for companies that fail to protect consumer data. At the federal level, the breach renewed calls for comprehensive data protection legislation, although such efforts have faced significant political hurdles.

The Target data breach also underscored the importance of a proactive and coordinated approach to cybersecurity. Organizations began to place greater emphasis on incident response planning, recognizing that timely detection and mitigation of breaches can significantly reduce their impact. This included the development of comprehensive incident response plans, regular training for employees on cybersecurity best practices, and the establishment of dedicated security operations centers (SOCs) to monitor and respond to threats in real-time.

In addition to technical measures, the breach highlighted the need for strong governance and oversight of cybersecurity practices. Boards of directors and senior executives became more engaged in cybersecurity issues, recognizing that data breaches can have severe financial and reputational consequences. This shift in perspective led to increased investment in cybersecurity initiatives and the appointment of chief information security officers (CISOs) to oversee organizational security efforts.

The Target data breach also had a lasting impact on consumer behavior and awareness of cybersecurity issues. Many consumers became more cautious about sharing their personal information online and began to take proactive steps to protect themselves, such as using strong, unique passwords for different accounts and regularly monitoring their financial statements for suspicious activity. The breach also highlighted the importance of consumer education and awareness campaigns to help individuals recognize and respond to potential security threats.

Chapter 13: Anthem Data Breach

The Anthem data breach of 2015 stands as one of the largest and most significant cybersecurity incidents in the history of the United States. Anthem Inc., a major health insurance provider, suffered a massive data breach that exposed the personal information of approximately 78.8 million current and former customers, as well as employees. The breach was discovered on January 27, 2015, but the attackers had been infiltrating Anthem's systems since at least December 10, 2014. This prolonged period of unauthorized access allowed the cybercriminals to collect a vast amount of sensitive data, which included names, dates of birth, social security numbers, addresses, phone numbers, email addresses, employment information, and income data.

The breach was particularly alarming because it did not involve credit card or medical information directly, which are often the primary targets in such attacks. Instead, the stolen data consisted of deeply personal identifiers that could be used for a range of malicious activities, from identity theft to sophisticated social engineering attacks. The attackers accessed Anthem's IT system via stolen credentials, which allowed them to move laterally within the network and extract large volumes of data without triggering immediate alarms.

Anthem discovered the breach when its security team noticed suspicious activity on its network. Upon investigation, they found that an unauthorized entity had been accessing and siphoning off data. The breach was publicly disclosed by Anthem on February 4, 2015. The announcement caused a significant public outcry, as millions of individuals suddenly faced the risk of identity theft and other forms of fraud. Anthem took swift action by notifying affected individuals, offering free credit monitoring and identity protection services for two years, and cooperating with federal investigators to understand the scope and source of the breach.

In the wake of the breach, Anthem faced intense scrutiny from regulatory bodies, including the Federal Bureau of Investigation (FBI) and the Department of Health and Human Services (HHS). The breach highlighted significant vulnerabilities in Anthem's cybersecurity defenses, prompting calls for better security practices across the healthcare industry. Subsequent investigations revealed that the attack likely originated from a foreign nation-state, with many cybersecurity experts attributing it to Chinese hackers. The sophistication of the attack suggested that it was not a typical criminal operation but rather a concerted effort to gather intelligence on a massive scale.

The financial impact of the breach on Anthem was substantial. The company faced numerous lawsuits, including class-action suits from affected customers who alleged that Anthem had failed to adequately protect their personal information. In 2017, Anthem agreed to a $115 million settlement to resolve these lawsuits, marking one of the largest data breach settlements in history. This settlement covered costs related to credit monitoring services, out-of-pocket expenses incurred by victims, and improvements to Anthem's cybersecurity measures.

Beyond the immediate financial and legal repercussions, the breach had long-term implications for Anthem's reputation and operations. It underscored the critical importance of cybersecurity in the healthcare sector, where sensitive personal and medical information is a prime target for cybercriminals. The breach served as a wake-up call for the entire industry, leading to increased investment in cybersecurity infrastructure and a heightened awareness of the need for robust data protection measures.

Anthem responded by overhauling its cybersecurity protocols. The company implemented advanced encryption for sensitive data, strengthened its network security measures, and conducted comprehensive security training for its employees. These efforts aimed to mitigate the risk of future breaches and restore trust among its customers. Additionally, Anthem worked closely with cybersecurity experts to continuously monitor and enhance its defenses against emerging threats.

The Anthem data breach also had broader policy implications. It contributed to the ongoing debate about the role of government and private sector collaboration in combating cyber threats. In response to the breach, lawmakers and regulators called for stricter data protection regulations and more stringent enforcement of existing laws. The incident highlighted the need for a unified approach to cybersecurity, involving not only individual companies but also industry-wide standards and government support.

The breach underscored the evolving nature of cyber threats and the increasing sophistication of cybercriminals. It demonstrated that even large, well-resourced organizations are vulnerable to determined attackers. This realization prompted many companies to reassess their cybersecurity strategies and prioritize the protection of personal data. The healthcare sector, in particular, recognized the need for a proactive stance on cybersecurity, given the high value of the data it holds.

In the years following the Anthem breach, there was a noticeable shift towards more integrated and comprehensive cybersecurity frameworks within the healthcare industry. Companies began adopting advanced technologies such as artificial intelligence and machine learning to detect and respond to threats in real-time. There was also a greater emphasis on collaboration and information sharing among organizations to collectively defend against cyber threats.

The Anthem data breach remains a pivotal moment in the history of cybersecurity, illustrating the far-reaching consequences of cyberattacks on personal data and the critical need for robust security measures. It serves as a case study for the importance of vigilance, preparedness, and continuous improvement in the face of an ever-changing threat landscape. As cyber threats continue to evolve, the lessons learned from the Anthem breach will continue to inform and shape cybersecurity practices and policies across industries.

Chapter 14: Ashley Madison Hack

The Ashley Madison hack of 2015 represents one of the most notorious and high-profile cybercrimes in the history of the internet. Ashley Madison, a website dedicated to facilitating extramarital affairs, operated under the slogan "Life is short. Have an affair." The platform promised discretion and anonymity for its users, who numbered in the millions worldwide. However, the breach exposed the intimate details of the website's clientele, leading to public embarrassment, personal crises, and, in some cases, tragic outcomes.

The hack was first made public on July 15, 2015, when a group calling itself the "Impact Team" claimed responsibility. The hackers announced that they had gained access to the user databases of Ashley Madison and its parent company, Avid Life Media (ALM). They threatened to release the personal information of Ashley Madison's users unless the website was taken down permanently. The demands specifically targeted Ashley Madison and another ALM site called Established Men, but the hackers did not seek financial gain; instead, they seemed motivated by a moralistic stance against the site's business model and its perceived promotion of infidelity.

ALM initially downplayed the severity of the breach and assured users that steps were being taken to secure the website and protect user data. However, on August 18, 2015, the Impact Team followed through on their threat and released approximately 10 gigabytes of data. This data dump included the personal details of over 30 million Ashley Madison users, encompassing names, addresses, phone numbers, email addresses, and partial credit card information. Additionally, the breach exposed transaction records, account details, and the messages exchanged between users.

The fallout from the data release was immediate and far-reaching. The public exposure of users' identities led to widespread humiliation and personal turmoil. Many users were outed as having accounts on

Ashley Madison, including public figures, politicians, and high-profile executives. The breach prompted numerous resignations and terminations from employment. In some tragic cases, individuals reportedly took their own lives due to the stress and shame associated with the exposure.

One of the most controversial aspects of the breach was the revelation that a significant portion of the accounts on Ashley Madison appeared to be fake. Investigations into the data suggested that many female profiles were actually bots or fictitious accounts created by the company to give the impression of a more balanced gender ratio. This added another layer of scandal to the breach, highlighting deceptive practices by ALM and further angering users who felt betrayed.

The legal repercussions were extensive. ALM faced multiple class-action lawsuits from affected users who claimed that the company had failed to protect their data adequately and had misled them about the level of security provided. The lawsuits also addressed the issue of the fake profiles and the company's overall ethical conduct. In 2017, ALM agreed to a settlement of $11.2 million to resolve the class-action lawsuits, though this was a fraction of the potential damages the company could have faced had the cases gone to trial.

The breach also led to regulatory scrutiny. The Federal Trade Commission (FTC) and the Office of the Privacy Commissioner of Canada conducted investigations into ALM's data security practices. The findings were damning, revealing that the company had inadequate security measures in place and had misrepresented its security capabilities to users. ALM agreed to implement more rigorous data protection measures and to undergo regular security audits as part of the settlements with these regulatory bodies.

The Ashley Madison hack had a profound impact on public perceptions of cybersecurity and privacy, especially concerning online dating and social networking platforms. It underscored the vulnerabilities inherent in storing sensitive personal information online and the potential consequences of data breaches. The incident also highlighted the ethical and moral complexities surrounding online anonymity and the promises made by companies to their users.

In the aftermath of the breach, there was a significant increase in the emphasis placed on cybersecurity across various industries. Companies became more vigilant about their data protection practices, investing in advanced security technologies and protocols to safeguard user information. The hack also spurred greater public awareness about the importance of personal data security and the risks associated with sharing sensitive information online.

On a societal level, the breach reignited debates about privacy, morality, and the implications of digital footprints. The exposure of Ashley Madison's users brought to light the often-hidden aspects of people's lives and the potential for digital platforms to impact real-world relationships and reputations. It raised questions about the ethics of businesses that profit from facilitating behavior that many consider morally dubious, as well as the responsibility of these businesses to protect their customers' privacy.

For cybersecurity professionals, the Ashley Madison hack became a case study in the importance of comprehensive security strategies and the potential risks posed by cybercriminals with a social or moral agenda. The incident demonstrated that cyber-attacks are not always financially motivated and that attackers can have a variety of motives, including ideological beliefs and desires to expose or disrupt certain practices.

The Ashley Madison hack remains a pivotal event in the history of cybercrime, illustrating the profound impact that data breaches can have on individuals and organizations alike. It serves as a reminder of the critical need for robust cybersecurity measures, transparent business practices, and a thoughtful approach to handling sensitive information. The lessons learned from this breach continue to influence the way companies approach data security and the ongoing efforts to protect personal privacy in an increasingly digital world.

Chapter 15: Bangladesh Bank Heist

The Bangladesh Bank Heist of 2016 stands as one of the most audacious and complex cybercrimes in financial history. This heist involved the theft of $81 million from the Bangladesh central bank's account at the Federal Reserve Bank of New York, executed through a sophisticated cyber-attack that exposed vulnerabilities in the global financial system. The incident highlighted the growing threats posed by cybercriminals and the need for enhanced security measures in the banking sector.

The heist began with the attackers gaining unauthorized access to Bangladesh Bank's systems. They infiltrated the bank's computer network using malware, which allowed them to observe the bank's activities and gather crucial information about its operations. This malware was likely introduced via spear-phishing emails sent to employees, which contained malicious attachments or links. Once inside the network, the attackers patiently monitored the bank's operations for several weeks or months, learning how to navigate the systems and timing their attack to avoid detection.

The attackers chose the weekend of February 4, 2016, to execute their plan, capitalizing on the fact that Bangladesh Bank was closed for the weekend, while the Federal Reserve Bank of New York would be open. This strategic timing minimized the chances of immediate detection. Using the stolen credentials, they initiated 35 fraudulent transfer requests from Bangladesh Bank's account at the New York Fed, totaling nearly $1 billion. The transfer requests were sent via the SWIFT network, a secure messaging system used by banks worldwide to execute financial transactions.

The majority of these transfer requests were flagged by the New York Fed's security systems, and only five transactions, amounting to $101 million, were processed. These funds were transferred to accounts in the Philippines and Sri Lanka. In Sri Lanka, a transaction of $20 million intended for a nonprofit organization was halted and reversed due to a typographical error in the beneficiary's name, which raised suspicions. However, $81 million transferred to accounts in the Philippines went through successfully and was quickly laundered through a complex network of casinos and money changers, making recovery extremely difficult.

The heist was discovered by Bangladesh Bank on the morning of February 5, 2016, when officials found discrepancies in their account balance. Immediate efforts were made to halt the transactions and recover the funds, but much of the money had already disappeared. The Bangladesh Bank notified the New York Fed and SWIFT, and the heist soon became public, drawing international attention.

Investigations into the heist revealed significant lapses in cybersecurity at Bangladesh Bank. The bank's systems were not properly secured, lacking basic protections such as firewalls and updated software. Additionally, the SWIFT messaging system, though generally secure, was compromised due to inadequate security practices at the bank. The attackers exploited these weaknesses to gain access and manipulate the transfer requests.

The response to the heist involved multiple agencies and countries, including Bangladesh, the United States, the Philippines, and international organizations like SWIFT. Forensic experts traced the origin of the malware to a server in North Korea, leading to speculation that the attack was orchestrated by the Lazarus Group, a hacking collective with ties to the North Korean government. The group was already known for its involvement in various cyber-attacks, including the 2014 Sony Pictures hack.

The Bangladesh Bank Heist had far-reaching implications for the global financial system. It exposed vulnerabilities in international banking infrastructure and highlighted the need for stronger cybersecurity measures. In response, SWIFT launched a customer security program aimed at improving the security of its network and member banks. This program included mandatory security controls, increased information sharing about threats, and enhanced support for banks to improve their defenses.

The incident also prompted banks worldwide to reevaluate their cybersecurity strategies. Financial institutions began investing more in cybersecurity technologies, conducting rigorous security audits, and training employees to recognize and respond to cyber threats. The heist underscored the importance of a multi-layered security approach, integrating both technological solutions and human vigilance to protect against sophisticated cyber-attacks.

In Bangladesh, the heist led to significant changes at the central bank. Several high-ranking officials resigned or were dismissed in the wake of the incident. The bank undertook a comprehensive overhaul of its IT systems, strengthening its cybersecurity measures and improving its operational protocols to prevent future breaches. The government also took steps to enhance national cybersecurity capabilities, recognizing the broader implications of the heist for national security and economic stability.

The Bangladesh Bank Heist remains a sobering reminder of the evolving nature of cybercrime and the persistent threats faced by the financial sector. It highlighted the need for continuous improvement in cybersecurity practices and international cooperation to combat cyber threats. The heist also emphasized the importance of timely detection and response, as the swift movement of stolen funds through global financial networks can make recovery efforts exceedingly challenging.

Despite the loss and the challenges posed by the heist, it also served as a catalyst for positive change. The financial industry became more aware of the risks associated with cyber threats and took proactive steps to enhance security. Governments and regulatory bodies around the world recognized the need for robust cybersecurity frameworks and increased their focus on protecting critical financial infrastructure.

The Bangladesh Bank Heist of 2016 is not just a story of loss but also a powerful lesson in the importance of vigilance, preparedness, and resilience in the face of cyber adversities. It continues to influence the way financial institutions approach cybersecurity, shaping policies and practices to safeguard the integrity of the global financial system. The heist is a testament to the fact that while cybercriminals may be innovative and persistent, the collective efforts of institutions, governments, and individuals can significantly strengthen defenses and mitigate risks in the digital age.

Chapter 16: DNC Email Leak

The DNC email leak of 2016 stands as a watershed moment in the intersection of cybersecurity, politics, and international relations. This cyber incident involved the unauthorized access and subsequent public release of thousands of emails from the Democratic National Committee (DNC), causing significant upheaval in the American political landscape. The leak not only influenced the 2016 U.S. presidential election but also underscored the growing threat of state-sponsored cyber operations.

The roots of the DNC email leak trace back to mid-2015, when the DNC's network was first infiltrated by cyber operatives. The attackers, later identified as Russian intelligence agencies GRU (Main Intelligence Directorate) and FSB (Federal Security Service), used spear-phishing emails to compromise the accounts of key DNC staffers. These emails contained links to malicious websites that mimicked legitimate services, tricking recipients into entering their credentials. Once inside the network, the attackers moved laterally, gaining access to email servers and other sensitive systems.

The attack went undetected for months, during which the hackers exfiltrated vast amounts of data. The intruders specifically targeted email accounts of high-ranking officials and compiled a trove of internal communications. This included emails from DNC Chairwoman Debbie Wasserman Schultz, communications director Luis Miranda, and other senior figures. The data extracted by the attackers encompassed strategy documents, donor information, and personal correspondences, providing a comprehensive view of the DNC's inner workings.

The breach came to light in April 2016 when the cybersecurity firm CrowdStrike was brought in to investigate unusual network activity. CrowdStrike quickly identified the presence of sophisticated malware linked to Russian intelligence agencies. Despite attempts to secure the network, the attackers had already accomplished their mission. In June 2016, a persona known as "Guccifer 2.0" claimed responsibility for the hack and began leaking documents to the media. Guccifer 2.0, purported to be a lone Romanian hacker, was later exposed as a front for the GRU.

The most significant release of emails occurred on July 22, 2016, just days before the Democratic National Convention. WikiLeaks published nearly 20,000 emails, revealing internal discussions and strategies. The content of the emails showed apparent bias within the DNC in favor of Hillary Clinton over Bernie Sanders during the primary elections. These revelations led to a public outcry and accusations of a rigged primary process, exacerbating divisions within the Democratic Party. The fallout was immediate and severe: Debbie Wasserman Schultz resigned as DNC chairwoman, and other officials faced intense scrutiny.

The timing and nature of the leaks raised suspicions of foreign interference aimed at undermining the credibility of the U.S. electoral process. The U.S. intelligence community, in a joint statement released in October 2016, officially attributed the hacks to Russian operatives. They concluded that the breach was part of a broader effort to interfere in the election, sow discord, and damage the Clinton campaign. This marked a significant moment in U.S.-Russia relations, as it highlighted the use of cyber tools as instruments of statecraft and influence.

The DNC email leak had profound implications for the 2016 presidential election. The constant media coverage of the leaked emails kept the DNC in a negative spotlight, distracting from the broader campaign messages and allowing the Trump campaign to capitalize on the controversy. The release of damaging information at critical junctures was perceived by many as an attempt to influence voter perceptions and outcomes. The scandal overshadowed the Democratic National Convention, which should have been a moment of unity and momentum for the Clinton campaign.

In response to the breach, the DNC took extensive measures to bolster its cybersecurity. They replaced outdated systems, implemented stronger authentication protocols, and conducted comprehensive training for staff on recognizing phishing attempts. The incident also prompted a broader reassessment of cybersecurity practices across political organizations. Both the Democratic and Republican parties, as well as other political entities, heightened their defenses against cyber threats, recognizing the critical importance of protecting sensitive information.

The repercussions of the DNC email leak extended beyond the immediate political fallout. It spurred a series of investigations and legislative actions aimed at understanding and countering foreign influence in U.S. elections. The FBI launched an investigation into the breach, and special counsel Robert Mueller was appointed to probe Russian interference in the 2016 election. Mueller's investigation confirmed the involvement of Russian intelligence in the DNC hack and detailed extensive efforts to disrupt the election through cyber operations and disinformation campaigns.

The incident also led to the indictment of 12 Russian intelligence officers by the U.S. Department of Justice in July 2018. These indictments provided detailed accounts of the methods used to breach the DNC network, the coordination between various actors, and the subsequent dissemination of stolen information. Although the indicted individuals were unlikely to face trial in the U.S., the indictments served as a public acknowledgment of the cyber intrusion and a formal attribution of responsibility.

On the international stage, the DNC email leak contributed to growing concerns about state-sponsored cyber activities and their impact on democratic processes. The incident underscored the need for international norms and agreements to govern state behavior in cyberspace. It also highlighted the importance of cybersecurity cooperation among nations to defend against common threats and uphold the integrity of democratic institutions.

The DNC email leak of 2016 remains a seminal event in the annals of cyber warfare, illustrating the profound impact that cyber operations can have on political processes and public trust. It serves as a cautionary tale of the vulnerabilities inherent in digital communications and the sophisticated tactics employed by state actors to exploit these weaknesses. The lessons learned from this breach continue to inform cybersecurity strategies and policies, emphasizing the need for vigilance, resilience, and international collaboration in an increasingly interconnected world.

The incident also left an indelible mark on the American political landscape. It deepened partisan divides, fueled conspiracy theories, and fostered a climate of mistrust and skepticism towards political institutions. The legacy of the DNC email leak is a stark reminder of the fragility of democratic processes in the face of evolving cyber threats and the critical importance of safeguarding the integrity of electoral systems against all forms of interference.

Chapter 17: Shadow Brokers

The Shadow Brokers saga, unfolding between 2016 and 2017, represents a pivotal and alarming chapter in the history of cyber espionage and cybersecurity. This mysterious group surfaced in August 2016, claiming to possess a trove of hacking tools and exploits allegedly stolen from the National Security Agency (NSA), one of the world's premier intelligence agencies. The Shadow Brokers' activities not only exposed the capabilities of state-sponsored cyber operations but also underscored the vulnerabilities inherent in even the most secure intelligence infrastructures.

The initial appearance of the Shadow Brokers was marked by a dramatic and cryptic announcement on various online platforms. The group claimed to have breached the Equation Group, a clandestine hacking team widely believed to be affiliated with the NSA. The Shadow Brokers offered samples of the stolen data to prove the authenticity of their claims, including a range of sophisticated hacking tools, exploits, and zero-day vulnerabilities that targeted widely used software and systems. They demanded a ransom in Bitcoin, threatening to auction the rest of the data to the highest bidder if their demands were not met.

The leaked tools were of extraordinary significance, as they demonstrated capabilities that had been kept secret and out of reach of most cyber actors. Among the released exploits were sophisticated mechanisms for compromising firewalls, routers, and other critical network infrastructure. This included exploits like "EPICBANANA," "JETPLOW," and "EXTRABACON," which targeted products from major vendors such as Cisco, Juniper, and Fortinet. The revelation of these tools posed immediate security risks, prompting emergency patches and security advisories from the affected companies.

The hacking community and cybersecurity experts were astonished by the quality and scope of the tools, which suggested they had originated from a highly advanced actor, consistent with the resources and capabilities of a state-sponsored entity like the NSA. The implications of the leak were profound, as it meant that these powerful tools could now be used by malicious actors worldwide, significantly raising the threat level for organizations across the globe.

As the Shadow Brokers continued to release more data in subsequent months, they maintained a provocative and taunting stance, issuing messages filled with broken English, cryptic references, and veiled threats. These communications suggested a sophisticated understanding of both technical and psychological warfare, aiming to sow confusion and fear within the cybersecurity community and the general public.

The group's activities took a significant turn in April 2017, when they released a new batch of tools, including the infamous "EternalBlue" exploit. EternalBlue exploited a vulnerability in the Windows Server Message Block (SMB) protocol, allowing remote code execution on vulnerable machines. This exploit proved to be extraordinarily damaging, as it was subsequently used in the WannaCry ransomware attack in May 2017. WannaCry spread rapidly across the globe, infecting hundreds of thousands of computers in over 150 countries, crippling hospitals, businesses, and government agencies. The attack highlighted the devastating potential of weaponized cyber tools in the wrong hands.

EternalBlue was also employed in the NotPetya attack in June 2017, which masqueraded as ransomware but was actually designed to cause maximum disruption and damage. NotPetya primarily targeted Ukraine but caused collateral damage worldwide, affecting major corporations and critical infrastructure. These incidents underscored the destructive power of the tools leaked by the Shadow Brokers and the far-reaching consequences of their disclosure.

The identity and motives of the Shadow Brokers remain shrouded in mystery. Various theories have been proposed, ranging from disgruntled insiders within the NSA to Russian state-sponsored actors seeking to undermine U.S. intelligence capabilities. The timing and nature of the leaks, coupled with the group's messaging, have fueled speculation about their origins and objectives. Some analysts believe the leaks were a form of retaliation for geopolitical tensions, while others suggest they were intended to expose and embarrass the NSA, showcasing its inability to secure its own tools.

The impact of the Shadow Brokers' leaks on the NSA and the broader intelligence community was profound. The breach revealed serious lapses in internal security and raised questions about the agency's ability to protect its most sensitive assets. It prompted a reevaluation of cybersecurity practices within the intelligence community and spurred efforts to enhance the security of critical cyber tools. The incident also led to increased scrutiny and debate over the stockpiling of zero-day vulnerabilities by intelligence agencies, with critics arguing that such practices pose significant risks if the tools fall into the wrong hands.

In response to the leaks, the NSA and other intelligence agencies faced intense pressure to improve their cyber defenses and accountability measures. The U.S. government also took steps to address the broader implications of the leaks, working with international partners to mitigate the threats posed by the exposed tools and to develop more robust defenses against similar future incidents. The Shadow Brokers episode highlighted the need for greater collaboration and information sharing between the public and private sectors to enhance collective cybersecurity resilience.

The Shadow Brokers saga also had significant ramifications for the cybersecurity industry. The disclosure of advanced hacking tools pushed security researchers and companies to innovate and develop new defensive technologies. It accelerated the adoption of advanced threat detection and response systems, as well as the deployment of more sophisticated encryption and authentication mechanisms. The incident underscored the importance of proactive security measures and the need for continuous monitoring and assessment of cyber threats.

Beyond the immediate security implications, the Shadow Brokers leak contributed to a broader understanding of the dynamics of cyber warfare and espionage. It illustrated the intricate and often hidden battles that take place in cyberspace, where state and non-state actors engage in complex operations to gain strategic advantages. The saga served as a stark reminder of the interconnectedness of global digital infrastructure and the shared responsibility to protect it from malicious actors.

The legacy of the Shadow Brokers is a complex one, marked by both the damage caused by the leaked tools and the advancements in cybersecurity practices that resulted from the incident. It stands as a cautionary tale of the potential consequences of cyber espionage and the critical need for robust security measures to safeguard sensitive information. The ongoing efforts to understand and mitigate the risks associated with state-sponsored cyber operations continue to shape the landscape of cybersecurity, informed by the lessons learned from the Shadow Brokers episode.

The Shadow Brokers' actions have left an indelible mark on the field of cybersecurity, illustrating the profound and far-reaching impact that a single breach can have on global security. The events of 2016 and 2017 serve as a testament to the evolving nature of cyber threats and the imperative for constant vigilance, innovation, and international cooperation to defend against the ever-present dangers in the digital age.

Chapter 18: Russian Election Interference

The Russian interference in the 2016 United States presidential election is one of the most significant and contentious events in recent political history. This complex operation, orchestrated by the Russian government, aimed to influence the election's outcome, sow discord within American society, and undermine confidence in democratic institutions. The interference involved a multifaceted strategy, including cyberattacks, disinformation campaigns, and the strategic use of social media to influence public opinion.

The origins of the interference trace back to the long-standing geopolitical rivalry between the United States and Russia. Under the leadership of Vladimir Putin, Russia sought to reassert its influence on the global stage and counter what it perceived as Western encroachment. The 2016 election presented an opportunity for Russia to achieve several objectives: weaken Hillary Clinton, whom Putin viewed as hostile to Russian interests, elevate Donald Trump, who had expressed more favorable views toward Russia, and erode public trust in the U.S. electoral process.

The first major component of the interference was a series of cyberattacks targeting various entities within the Democratic Party. In early 2016, Russian military intelligence agency GRU launched a spear-phishing campaign against the Democratic National Committee (DNC) and the Democratic Congressional Campaign Committee (DCCC). These attacks involved sending emails that appeared legitimate but contained malicious links, which, when clicked, allowed the attackers to gain access to the recipients' email accounts. The GRU successfully infiltrated the DNC's network, exfiltrating a large cache of emails and other sensitive documents.

The stolen data was subsequently leaked to the public in two major phases. The first phase involved the online persona known as "Guccifer 2.0," who claimed to be a lone Romanian hacker but was later revealed to be a front for the GRU. Guccifer 2.0 released a series of documents, including internal DNC communications, which were picked up by media outlets and used to fuel narratives of corruption and favoritism within the Democratic Party. The second phase saw the data handed over to WikiLeaks, which published a trove of emails just days before the Democratic National Convention in July 2016. The release of these emails caused a significant scandal, leading to the resignation of DNC Chairwoman Debbie Wasserman Schultz and damaging the party's unity at a critical moment in the campaign.

In addition to cyberattacks, the Russian interference campaign employed a sophisticated disinformation strategy through social media platforms. The Internet Research Agency (IRA), a Kremlin-linked "troll farm," played a central role in this effort. The IRA created thousands of fake social media accounts that masqueraded as American citizens, including political activists, journalists, and ordinary users. These accounts were used to amplify divisive content, spread conspiracy theories, and promote inflammatory narratives on platforms like Facebook, Twitter, and Instagram.

The IRA's activities were designed to exploit existing social and political divisions in the United States. They targeted issues such as race relations, immigration, gun control, and political corruption, crafting content that resonated with various segments of the American electorate. By creating and promoting content that appealed to both the far-left and far-right, the IRA sought to deepen polarization and create a sense of chaos and mistrust. Notably, the IRA organized and promoted real-world events, such as protests and rallies, sometimes even coordinating events on opposing sides of contentious issues to provoke confrontations.

The disinformation campaign was not limited to social media. Russian state-sponsored media outlets, such as RT (formerly Russia Today) and Sputnik, also played a role in disseminating misleading narratives and conspiracy theories. These outlets often framed their coverage to cast doubt on the integrity of the electoral process and to portray the United States as a country in decline and riddled with corruption. This messaging was intended to weaken the credibility of American democratic institutions and to bolster the perception of Russian strength and stability.

As the election drew closer, the intensity of Russian interference efforts increased. The GRU targeted election infrastructure in various states, attempting to probe voter registration databases and other systems. While there is no evidence that these efforts resulted in any actual alteration of votes or voter data, the attempts added to the atmosphere of uncertainty and concern about the security of the election.

The impact of the Russian interference on the election outcome is a matter of ongoing debate. While it is impossible to quantify precisely how much influence the campaign had on voters' decisions, it is clear that the interference introduced significant disruptions. The hacked emails and disinformation campaigns created a barrage of negative publicity for Hillary Clinton and the Democratic Party, which may have swayed some undecided voters. Additionally, the amplification of divisive content likely contributed to the overall polarization and mistrust that characterized the 2016 election.

In the aftermath of the election, various investigations were launched to understand the extent and impact of the Russian interference. The most prominent of these was the investigation led by Special Counsel Robert Mueller, appointed in May 2017. Mueller's investigation sought to uncover the full scope of the Russian operations and to determine whether there was any coordination between the Trump campaign and Russian operatives.

The Mueller Report, released in April 2019, confirmed that Russia had engaged in a "sweeping and systematic" effort to influence the 2016 election. The report detailed the cyberattacks on the DNC, the disinformation campaigns carried out by the IRA, and the attempts to infiltrate state election systems. It also identified multiple instances of interactions between Trump campaign associates and individuals linked to the Russian government. However, the report did not establish that the Trump campaign had conspired or coordinated with the Russian government in its interference activities.

The release of the Mueller Report sparked significant political controversy and debate. Supporters of President Trump seized on the finding of no conspiracy to claim exoneration, while critics argued that the report detailed numerous instances of obstruction of justice that warranted further investigation and potential legal consequences. The report also made several recommendations for improving election security and addressing foreign interference, many of which have been the subject of legislative and administrative action in subsequent years.

The Russian interference in the 2016 election has had enduring implications for American politics and international relations. It has heightened awareness of the vulnerabilities in the electoral process and the need for robust cybersecurity measures. It has also underscored the challenges of combating disinformation in an era of social media and digital communication. The incident has prompted a reevaluation of how democracies can protect themselves from external interference while maintaining the openness and transparency that are central to their functioning.

On a geopolitical level, the interference has further strained relations between the United States and Russia. The U.S. government has imposed sanctions on Russian individuals and entities involved in the interference and has taken steps to bolster its defenses against future cyber threats. The incident has also led to increased cooperation among Western countries to address the shared threat of state-sponsored cyber operations.

The lessons of the 2016 Russian election interference continue to shape the landscape of cybersecurity and electoral integrity. As technology evolves and new threats emerge, the experience of 2016 serves as a cautionary tale of the need for vigilance, resilience, and proactive measures to safeguard democracy. The ongoing efforts to address these challenges reflect a commitment to protecting the fundamental principles of free and fair elections and to ensuring that the democratic process remains resilient in the face of ever-changing threats.

Chapter 19: Uber Data Breach

The Uber data breach of 2016 is a significant example of corporate mismanagement and failure to protect sensitive customer and driver information. This breach not only exposed the personal data of millions but also highlighted severe shortcomings in Uber's approach to cybersecurity and transparency. The incident has had far-reaching implications for the company and has influenced regulatory practices and public perception of data security.

In October 2016, Uber, one of the world's largest ride-sharing companies, suffered a major data breach that compromised the personal information of approximately 57 million users and drivers worldwide. The breach included names, email addresses, and phone numbers of 50 million riders, as well as the personal information of 7 million drivers, including about 600,000 U.S. driver's license numbers. The attackers also accessed internal Uber data stored on third-party cloud services.

The breach began when hackers managed to gain access to Uber's data stored on Amazon Web Services (AWS). They obtained login credentials to Uber's AWS account, reportedly found on a private GitHub repository used by Uber's engineers. GitHub is a platform for version control and collaborative development, but storing sensitive data such as login credentials in code repositories is a critical security misstep. Once inside the AWS account, the hackers discovered and exfiltrated a vast amount of sensitive data.

Uber's initial response to the breach was highly controversial. Rather than disclosing the incident to affected individuals and regulatory authorities as required by law, Uber chose to cover it up. The company paid the hackers $100,000 to delete the stolen data and keep the breach confidential. Uber used its bug bounty program to facilitate the payment, which is typically intended to reward ethical hackers who report security vulnerabilities responsibly. By disguising the ransom payment as a bug bounty reward, Uber attempted to mask the severity of the incident.

The decision to conceal the breach was made by then-CEO Travis Kalanick and Chief Security Officer Joe Sullivan. Sullivan was instrumental in orchestrating the payment to the hackers and ensuring the breach remained hidden. However, Uber's strategy began to unravel as the company faced increasing scrutiny over its business practices and internal culture, which was often described as aggressive and unaccountable.

The breach and subsequent cover-up were exposed in November 2017, more than a year after the incident occurred. Uber's new CEO, Dara Khosrowshahi, who took over in August 2017 following Kalanick's resignation amid numerous controversies, publicly disclosed the breach and the company's response to it. Khosrowshahi's admission revealed the extent of the data compromise and the deliberate efforts to keep it from the public.

The revelation of the breach and its concealment led to widespread outrage and significant legal and financial repercussions for Uber. The company faced multiple lawsuits from affected users and drivers, alleging negligence and violation of consumer protection laws. Additionally, Uber became the subject of investigations by regulatory authorities in the United

States and other countries. The Federal Trade Commission (FTC) launched an investigation, and state attorneys general from various states pursued legal action against the company. Uber was eventually fined and had to settle various lawsuits, agreeing to more stringent data security practices and oversight.

The breach and its cover-up also had significant implications for Uber's leadership and corporate governance. Joe Sullivan, the Chief Security Officer who orchestrated the payment to the hackers, was fired. In addition to Sullivan's termination, several other high-ranking executives left the company as part of a broader shake-up aimed at addressing Uber's cultural and ethical issues. The scandal severely damaged Uber's reputation, which had already been tarnished by previous controversies, including allegations of sexual harassment and a toxic workplace culture.

From a cybersecurity perspective, the Uber data breach highlighted several critical failures. Firstly, the incident underscored the importance of secure credential management. Uber's decision to store AWS login credentials in a GitHub repository, accessible to anyone with access to the repository, was a glaring vulnerability. This practice violated basic cybersecurity principles, which dictate that sensitive information such as access credentials should be stored securely, preferably using encrypted storage solutions and stringent access controls.

Secondly, the breach emphasized the need for robust incident response strategies. Uber's initial response to the breach, involving a secret payment to the hackers and a cover-up, was not only unethical but also legally questionable. Effective incident response requires timely detection, thorough investigation, and prompt disclosure to affected parties and regulatory authorities. Transparency is crucial in maintaining public trust and complying with legal obligations. Uber's failure to disclose the breach in a timely manner exacerbated the situation, leading to severe legal and financial consequences.

Furthermore, the breach highlighted the risks associated with third-party services. Uber's reliance on AWS for data storage meant that any compromise of their AWS credentials exposed a significant amount of sensitive data. Organizations must implement stringent security measures when using third-party services, including regular audits, secure configuration management, and continuous monitoring for unauthorized access. Multi-factor authentication (MFA) and the principle of least privilege are also essential practices to minimize the risk of unauthorized access to critical systems.

The fallout from the Uber data breach extended beyond the company, influencing broader regulatory practices and public awareness of data security. The incident underscored the need for stronger data protection regulations and more aggressive enforcement of existing laws. In the United States, the breach contributed to calls for more comprehensive federal data protection legislation, complementing state-level initiatives such as the California Consumer Privacy Act (CCPA).

Internationally, the breach reinforced the importance of the General Data Protection Regulation (GDPR) in the European Union, which came into effect in May 2018. GDPR mandates stringent data protection requirements and imposes significant penalties for non-compliance, including failure to report data breaches promptly. The Uber incident served as a cautionary tale for other companies, highlighting the severe repercussions of inadequate data security and transparency.

In the aftermath of the breach, Uber undertook significant efforts to improve its cybersecurity posture and rebuild trust with its users and drivers. Under Dara Khosrowshahi's leadership, the company implemented a series of reforms aimed at enhancing data security, transparency, and corporate governance. Uber hired a new Chief Information Security Officer (CISO), expanded its security team, and invested in advanced security technologies and practices.

Uber also revised its incident response policies to ensure timely detection and reporting of security incidents. The company committed to regular security audits and assessments to identify and address vulnerabilities proactively. Additionally, Uber enhanced its bug bounty program, encouraging ethical hackers to report vulnerabilities responsibly and rewarding them appropriately.

The Uber data breach of 2016 serves as a stark reminder of the critical importance of cybersecurity and ethical corporate practices. The incident highlighted the vulnerabilities that can arise from poor credential management, inadequate incident response, and reliance on third-party services. It also underscored the necessity of transparency and prompt disclosure in maintaining public trust and complying with legal requirements.

For the broader business community, the breach reinforced the imperative to prioritize data security and implement robust safeguards to protect sensitive information. Organizations must adopt a holistic approach to cybersecurity, encompassing technical defenses, employee training, and governance frameworks. Continuous improvement and adaptation to evolving threats are essential to mitigate the risk of data breaches and ensure the protection of user and customer data.

The legacy of the Uber data breach continues to influence discussions on data security and corporate accountability. It stands as a cautionary tale for companies worldwide, illustrating the severe consequences of failing to protect sensitive information and the importance of ethical decision-making in times of crisis. As cyber threats continue to evolve, the lessons learned from the Uber breach remain relevant, guiding efforts to enhance security practices and safeguard the digital ecosystem.

Chapter 20: Mirai Botnet

The Mirai botnet, which emerged in 2016, is one of the most infamous examples of a large-scale cyber-attack utilizing a network of compromised devices. This botnet leveraged Internet of Things (IoT) devices, which often had poor security measures, to launch devastating Distributed Denial of Service (DDoS) attacks, impacting major websites and internet services. The Mirai botnet's story is a profound example of the growing threats in cybersecurity posed by the proliferation of interconnected devices.

Mirai, which means "future" in Japanese, was first discovered in August 2016 by MalwareMustDie, a white-hat security research group. The botnet specifically targeted IoT devices, including routers, security cameras, and digital video recorders, which often had default usernames and passwords that were rarely changed by users. By exploiting these weak security settings, Mirai was able to co-opt a vast number of devices into its botnet.

The creators of Mirai, later identified as Paras Jha, Josiah White, and Dalton Norman, designed the malware to scan the internet for vulnerable IoT devices, using a list of default credentials to gain control over them. Once infected, the devices would report back to command-and-control (C2) servers, where they could be used to coordinate and launch large-scale DDoS attacks. These attacks would flood target servers with traffic, overwhelming their capacity to process legitimate requests and effectively taking them offline.

One of the earliest and most significant attacks orchestrated by the Mirai botnet occurred on September 20, 2016. The target was the website of cybersecurity journalist Brian Krebs, known for his investigative work on cybercrime. The DDoS attack against Krebs' site was massive, reaching traffic volumes of 620 gigabits per second (Gbps), making it one of the largest such attacks at the time. The sheer scale of the attack forced Akamai, Krebs' DDoS mitigation service provider, to stop providing protection, temporarily taking the site offline.

However, the most impactful attack attributed to the Mirai botnet took place on October 21, 2016, targeting Dyn, a major DNS (Domain Name System) provider. Dyn's services are critical for resolving internet domain names into IP addresses, a fundamental process that underpins internet functionality. By targeting Dyn, the attackers effectively disrupted access to many popular websites and online services, including Twitter, Netflix, Reddit, CNN, and The Guardian. This attack, peaking at 1.2 terabits per second (Tbps), highlighted the potential for IoT botnets to cause widespread disruption across the internet.

The Dyn attack was a wake-up call for the cybersecurity community and the general public, underscoring the vulnerabilities inherent in the rapidly expanding IoT ecosystem. The botnet's ability to enlist a diverse array of devices into its ranks demonstrated the ease with which attackers could exploit the weak security of many consumer products. This event spurred increased scrutiny on the security practices of IoT device manufacturers, many of whom were criticized for prioritizing convenience and cost over robust security features.

Following the Dyn attack, law enforcement agencies and cybersecurity researchers intensified their efforts to trace the origins of Mirai and its operators. In December 2017, the U.S. Department of Justice announced the guilty pleas of Paras Jha, Josiah White, and Dalton Norman. The trio admitted to creating and deploying Mirai, initially to use it for DDoS attacks against their Minecraft competitors. They then decided to release the Mirai source code publicly in September 2016, which led to numerous copycat attacks and further proliferation of the botnet.

The release of Mirai's source code proved to be a significant turning point. It enabled other malicious actors to create their own variants of the botnet, leading to a surge in DDoS attacks worldwide. Some of these variants incorporated new features and targeted additional vulnerabilities, further complicating efforts to mitigate the threat. For instance, subsequent iterations of Mirai included capabilities to exploit vulnerabilities in more sophisticated devices and systems, not just those with default credentials.

The widespread impact of the Mirai botnet spurred various responses aimed at enhancing IoT security. Governments, industry groups, and cybersecurity professionals began advocating for stricter security standards and practices for IoT devices. Recommendations included requiring unique default passwords, implementing automatic security updates, and providing clearer guidelines for users on how to secure their devices.

The U.S. government took steps to address the issue through legislation and regulatory measures. The IoT Cybersecurity Improvement Act of 2020, for example, mandated that devices purchased by federal agencies meet minimum security requirements, including secure default settings and the ability to receive updates. This legislation aimed to set a benchmark for IoT security practices, encouraging manufacturers to adopt better security measures across their products.

Industry organizations also responded by developing security frameworks and guidelines for IoT devices. The Internet Engineering Task Force (IETF), for instance, worked on standards to improve IoT security protocols, such as ensuring secure boot processes, encrypted communications, and device authentication. The Online Trust Alliance (OTA), a non-profit organization focused on enhancing online trust and security, published IoT security and privacy principles to guide manufacturers in designing more secure products.

Despite these efforts, the challenge of securing IoT devices remains significant. The sheer diversity of IoT products, coupled with the varying levels of technical expertise among manufacturers and users, makes it difficult to establish and enforce uniform security standards.

Additionally, the global nature of IoT manufacturing and distribution complicates regulatory efforts, as different regions may have different standards and enforcement capabilities.

The Mirai botnet incident also highlighted the need for improved DDoS mitigation strategies. Service providers and network operators have since invested in more robust defenses, such as deploying advanced traffic filtering and anomaly detection systems, increasing bandwidth capacity, and collaborating with other entities to share threat intelligence. These measures aim to enhance the resilience of internet infrastructure against large-scale DDoS attacks.

In the wake of Mirai, the cybersecurity community has continued to evolve its approach to combating botnets and other cyber threats. Efforts include better threat intelligence sharing, collaborative defense initiatives, and public awareness campaigns to educate users about securing their devices. Researchers and cybersecurity firms regularly monitor for new botnet activities and work to develop tools and techniques to dismantle them before they can cause significant harm.

The legacy of the Mirai botnet is a cautionary tale about the vulnerabilities that accompany technological advancement and the interconnected nature of modern devices. It underscores the importance of proactive security measures and the need for a collective effort among manufacturers, users, policymakers, and cybersecurity professionals to protect the digital ecosystem. As the number of IoT devices continues to grow, the lessons learned from Mirai remain relevant, reminding us of the critical importance of securing our increasingly connected world.

Chapter 21: CCleaner Malware Attack

The CCleaner malware attack of 2017 is a notable example of a supply chain attack, where cybercriminals compromise a trusted software vendor to distribute malicious software to its users. This incident underscores the vulnerabilities inherent in the software development and distribution process and highlights the far-reaching implications of such attacks on both consumers and businesses.

CCleaner is a popular utility program developed by Piriform, a subsidiary of Avast, designed to optimize computer performance by cleaning up unnecessary files and managing system settings. The software, with millions of users worldwide, became the unwitting vehicle for distributing a sophisticated malware campaign.

In September 2017, researchers from Cisco Talos and Morphisec discovered that the CCleaner version 5.33.6162, released in August 2017, and CCleaner Cloud version 1.07.3191 had been compromised. The attack involved injecting a malicious payload into the software's installation packages, which were then distributed through the official CCleaner website. Users who downloaded and installed these versions of CCleaner inadvertently introduced malware into their systems.

The compromised versions of CCleaner contained a multi-stage malware payload. The first stage, embedded within the software's legitimate code, executed upon installation. This stage collected information about the infected system, including IP addresses, list of installed programs, running processes, network adapters, and other system details. The collected data was then transmitted to command-and-control (C2) servers controlled by the attackers.

The second stage of the malware was more selective and sophisticated. Based on the data gathered during the first stage, the attackers chose specific targets for further exploitation. These targets included high-profile technology companies such as Microsoft, Intel, Google, Cisco, and others. For these selected targets, the malware downloaded and executed a second-stage payload designed to establish a persistent backdoor in the infected systems. This backdoor allowed the attackers to maintain long-term access to the compromised networks, potentially for conducting espionage, data theft, or further malicious activities.

One of the notable aspects of the CCleaner malware attack was its sophisticated targeting and execution. The attackers demonstrated significant technical expertise and strategic planning, indicating that this was not the work of ordinary cybercriminals. Instead, the nature of the attack suggested the involvement of a well-resourced and highly skilled group, possibly state-sponsored actors.

Investigations into the CCleaner malware attack revealed that the initial compromise likely occurred at Piriform's development environment. The attackers managed to infiltrate the build server used to compile and package the CCleaner software. By compromising this server, they were able to inject the malicious code directly into the software during the development process, ensuring that the malware was signed with a valid digital certificate and appeared legitimate to users and security software.

The use of valid digital certificates was a critical factor in the success of the attack. Digital certificates are used to verify the authenticity of software, assuring users that the software comes from a trusted source and has not been tampered with. By signing the compromised versions of CCleaner with a valid certificate, the attackers bypassed many security measures, as the software appeared legitimate and trustworthy.

The response to the discovery of the malware was swift. Piriform and Avast worked closely with law enforcement and cybersecurity experts to investigate the breach, identify the affected versions, and mitigate the threat. They released updated versions of CCleaner without the malicious code and advised users to upgrade immediately. Additionally, they revoked the compromised digital certificates to prevent further distribution of the infected software.

Despite the quick response, the impact of the CCleaner malware attack was significant. Over 2.27 million users downloaded the compromised version of CCleaner, and while not all of these installations resulted in the second-stage infection, the attack nonetheless represented a massive breach of trust. The incident raised serious concerns about the security of the software supply chain and the potential for similar attacks in the future.

The CCleaner malware attack prompted widespread discussions within the cybersecurity community about the need for more robust security practices in software development and distribution. Supply chain attacks are particularly challenging to defend against because they exploit trusted relationships and established processes. As seen in the CCleaner case, even well-known and reputable software can become a vector for malware if the development process is compromised.

In response to the attack, companies and security professionals have emphasized the importance of securing the software supply chain. This includes implementing stringent security measures at every stage of software development, from coding and testing to packaging and distribution. Practices such as code signing, regular security audits, and the use of secure build environments are crucial in preventing unauthorized modifications to software.

Additionally, the incident highlighted the need for improved threat detection and response capabilities. Advanced threat detection systems that can identify anomalous behavior, even in software that appears legitimate, are essential in mitigating the risk of supply chain attacks. Collaborative efforts between software vendors, security researchers, and law enforcement are also critical in quickly identifying and responding to such threats.

The CCleaner malware attack also underscored the importance of user awareness and proactive security measures. Users are encouraged to regularly update their software, use reputable security solutions, and be cautious about the software they install. In the case of CCleaner, timely updates to the latest versions helped mitigate the impact of the attack for many users.

In the broader context, the CCleaner malware attack is a stark reminder of the evolving threat landscape and the increasing sophistication of cyber adversaries. As technology continues to advance and the digital ecosystem becomes more interconnected, the potential attack surface for cybercriminals expands. Organizations must remain vigilant and adopt a multi-layered approach to security, encompassing not only technical defenses but also robust policies, procedures, and awareness programs.

The long-term implications of the CCleaner malware attack continue to influence cybersecurity practices and policies. Governments and regulatory bodies have taken note of the risks associated with supply chain attacks and are considering measures to enhance the security of critical infrastructure and software systems. The incident serves as a case study in the importance of securing the entire software lifecycle and the need for continuous improvement in cybersecurity practices.

Chapter 22: Equifax Data Breach

The Equifax data breach of 2017 stands as one of the most significant and far-reaching cyber incidents in history. It highlighted vulnerabilities in data security practices and underscored the critical importance of protecting sensitive personal information. Equifax, one of the three major consumer credit reporting agencies in the United States, experienced a breach that exposed the personal information of approximately 147.9 million people, a staggering figure considering the U.S. population at the time. This breach not only compromised individuals' private data but also eroded trust in institutions responsible for safeguarding such information.

The breach occurred between mid-May and July 2017, but it wasn't publicly disclosed until September 7, 2017. During this period, attackers exploited a vulnerability in a web application framework known as Apache Struts, a tool commonly used in enterprise web applications. This specific vulnerability had been identified and a patch had been released by Apache in March 2017. However, Equifax failed to apply the patch in a timely manner, leaving their systems exposed to attack. The attackers used this vulnerability to gain access to Equifax's servers, where they were able to extract vast amounts of personal data over the course of several months.

The data compromised in the breach included a variety of sensitive information: names, social security numbers, birth dates, addresses, and in some cases, driver's license numbers. Additionally, around 209,000 individuals had their credit card details exposed, and documents containing personally identifiable information (PII) for approximately 182,000 people were also compromised. The breadth of data stolen made this breach particularly severe, as it provided a comprehensive set of details that could be used for identity theft and fraud on a massive scale.

The aftermath of the breach was immediate and profound. Equifax faced intense scrutiny from government agencies, consumer protection groups, and the public. The company was criticized for its delayed response and for its handling of the breach disclosure. Initially, Equifax offered a year of free credit monitoring to those affected, but the offer was criticized because signing up for the service initially included a clause that could be interpreted as waiving the right to sue the company. Public backlash led to Equifax removing this clause and extending the monitoring offer to all U.S. consumers.

In the wake of the breach, multiple investigations were launched. The U.S. Congress conducted hearings where Equifax executives were questioned about the company's data security practices and the specifics of the breach. The Federal Trade Commission (FTC) also investigated, eventually resulting in a settlement where Equifax agreed to pay up to $700 million. This settlement included a fund to provide credit monitoring services, reimburse victims for financial losses, and cover the costs of related identity restoration services. Additionally, Equifax was required to implement more robust security measures to prevent future breaches.

The Equifax data breach had widespread implications for the credit reporting industry and data security practices more broadly. It highlighted the critical need for timely patch management and rigorous cybersecurity protocols. The breach exposed significant weaknesses in Equifax's approach to security, including inadequate encryption practices, insufficient network segmentation, and poor overall vulnerability management. These shortcomings were indicative of broader industry issues, prompting calls for more stringent regulations and oversight.

Beyond the immediate impact on Equifax and its customers, the breach also raised awareness about the risks associated with data aggregation and the storage of personal information by large organizations. Consumers became more aware of the potential dangers of having their information stored by third parties, leading to increased demand for stronger data protection laws. In response to this growing concern, lawmakers and regulators around the world began to push for more comprehensive data protection regulations.

One of the most notable legislative responses to data breaches like that of Equifax was the introduction of the General Data Protection Regulation (GDPR) in the European Union, which came into effect in May 2018. While not a direct result of the Equifax breach, the timing and scope of GDPR highlighted a global trend towards more rigorous data protection standards. The regulation imposed strict requirements on how companies collect, store, and manage personal data, and it provided substantial penalties for non-compliance.

The Equifax breach also served as a case study in the importance of incident response and crisis management. Equifax's handling of the breach disclosure, communication with the public, and its subsequent actions were widely criticized. This highlighted the need for companies to have robust incident response plans in place and to communicate transparently and effectively in the aftermath of a breach. Equifax's failure to do so exacerbated the damage to its reputation and underscored the importance of being prepared for cyber incidents.

In terms of financial impact, the breach had significant consequences for Equifax. The company's stock price plummeted in the immediate aftermath of the breach's disclosure, losing over a third of its value. Equifax also faced numerous lawsuits, including class-action lawsuits from consumers and shareholder derivative suits. These legal challenges and the associated financial liabilities underscored the high costs of data breaches, not just in terms of direct financial losses but also in terms of long-term reputational damage.

For individuals affected by the breach, the consequences were potentially severe. The information stolen in the breach could be used by cybercriminals to commit a wide range of fraudulent activities, including opening new credit accounts, filing false tax returns, and even applying for loans or government benefits in the names of victims. The long-term impact of such fraud can be devastating, as it can take years for individuals to fully recover from identity theft and restore their financial reputations.

In the broader context of cybersecurity, the Equifax breach underscored the evolving nature of cyber threats and the increasing sophistication of cybercriminals. It highlighted the fact that even large, well-established companies with significant resources can fall victim to cyber-attacks if they do not maintain rigorous security practices. The breach also illustrated the interconnected nature of modern data ecosystems, where a breach at one organization can have far-reaching implications for millions of individuals and other businesses.

Chapter 23: WannaCry Ransomware Attack

The WannaCry ransomware attack of May 2017 represents one of the most significant and widespread cyberattacks in history, affecting hundreds of thousands of computers across more than 150 countries within just a few days. The attack, which began on May 12, 2017, was a stark demonstration of the vulnerabilities in global cybersecurity infrastructures and highlighted the potential for malicious software to cause massive disruption on an international scale. WannaCry exploited a critical vulnerability in Windows operating systems, underscoring the importance of timely software updates and robust cybersecurity practices.

WannaCry, also known as WannaCrypt, WanaCrypt0r 2.0, or simply WCry, is a type of ransomware, a form of malicious software designed to block access to a computer system until a sum of money is paid. The ransomware targeted computers running Microsoft Windows by encrypting files and demanding a ransom payment in Bitcoin to unlock them. It specifically exploited a security flaw in Microsoft's Server Message Block (SMB) protocol, a vulnerability that had been discovered by the National Security Agency (NSA) in the United States and was part of a suite of exploits, codenamed "EternalBlue," that were leaked online by a hacking group known as the Shadow Brokers in April 2017.

The rapid spread of WannaCry was facilitated by its worm-like capabilities, which allowed it to propagate across networks autonomously without requiring user interaction. Once a single computer was infected, WannaCry used the EternalBlue exploit to scan and infect other vulnerable machines on the same network, leading to a rapid and uncontrolled proliferation of the ransomware. This ability to spread independently across networks distinguished WannaCry from other types of ransomwares and significantly amplified its impact.

The initial infection vector for WannaCry is believed to have been phishing emails, a common tactic for distributing malware. These emails contained malicious attachments or links that, when opened, would install the ransomware on the user's computer. From there, WannaCry would begin encrypting files and display a ransom note demanding a payment of $300 in Bitcoin, which would double to $600 if not paid within three days. The ransom note also threatened to delete the encrypted files if the ransom was not paid within seven days, adding further pressure on victims to comply with the attackers' demands.

The attack had devastating effects on numerous sectors, including healthcare, transportation, telecommunications, and logistics. One of the most notable victims was the United Kingdom's National Health Service (NHS), which saw its operations severely disrupted as computers across its network were locked by the ransomware. Hospitals and clinics were forced to cancel appointments, delay surgeries, and turn away patients due to the inability to access vital medical records and systems. This disruption underscored the critical importance of cybersecurity in healthcare, where system downtime can have life-threatening consequences.

In addition to the NHS, other significant organizations and entities affected by the WannaCry attack included FedEx, Deutsche Bahn, the Russian Interior Ministry, and several universities and businesses across Asia and Europe. The attack's global reach and the high-profile nature of many of its victims drew widespread media attention and raised public awareness about the threats posed by ransomware and other forms of cybercrime.

The response to the WannaCry outbreak was swift and multifaceted. Cybersecurity experts, researchers, and organizations around the world scrambled to understand the nature of the attack and to mitigate its effects. One of the key developments in the response came from a British cybersecurity researcher known by the pseudonym MalwareTech. By registering a specific domain name found within the ransomware's code, MalwareTech inadvertently triggered a kill switch that halted the further spread of WannaCry. This domain registration effectively disabled the ransomware's ability to propagate, providing a temporary respite and allowing affected organizations to address the damage.

Despite the discovery of the kill switch, the attack continued to have a significant impact due to the large number of computers that had already been infected. Organizations scrambled to patch their systems and restore encrypted files, but many victims, particularly those with inadequate backup systems or outdated software, faced considerable challenges in recovering from the attack. The widespread nature of the infection also prompted an urgent review of cybersecurity practices across multiple sectors and highlighted the need for improved defenses against such attacks.

In the wake of the WannaCry attack, Microsoft released a series of patches and updates to address the vulnerability exploited by the ransomware. This included an unprecedented decision to issue patches for unsupported versions of Windows, such as Windows XP, which had not received regular security updates for several years. The decision to patch these older systems reflected the severity of the threat posed by WannaCry and the need to protect as many users as possible from its effects.

The WannaCry attack also had significant implications for the broader cybersecurity landscape. It underscored the importance of timely software updates and the dangers of relying on outdated systems that are no longer supported by vendors. The attack highlighted the critical need for organizations to maintain robust backup systems and to implement comprehensive cybersecurity policies that include regular vulnerability assessments, employee training, and incident response planning.

Furthermore, the attack raised important questions about the role of government agencies in cybersecurity. The fact that WannaCry exploited a vulnerability discovered by the NSA and later leaked to the public sparked a debate about the responsibilities of intelligence agencies in disclosing such vulnerabilities to vendors and the broader public. Critics argued that the NSA should have informed Microsoft about the flaw sooner, allowing the company to develop and distribute a patch before the vulnerability could be exploited by malicious actors.

The WannaCry attack also prompted a re-evaluation of international cooperation in addressing cyber threats. Given the global nature of the attack and its impact across multiple countries, it became clear that effective responses to such incidents require coordinated efforts and information sharing among governments, private sector organizations, and cybersecurity experts. The attack highlighted the need for a more proactive approach to cyber defense, including the development of international norms and agreements aimed at preventing and mitigating the impact of cyber-attacks.

In terms of financial impact, the WannaCry attack caused billions of dollars in damages. The costs included not only the ransom payments made by some victims but also the expenses associated with restoring systems, lost productivity, and the broader economic impact of the disruption. For many organizations, the attack served as a wake-up call about the financial risks associated with cybersecurity threats and the importance of investing in effective security measures to protect against future incidents.

Chapter 24: NotPetya Attack

The NotPetya attack of 2017 stands as one of the most devastating cyberattacks in history, characterized by its extraordinary scale, sophisticated nature, and the profound impact it had on global businesses and infrastructure. Occurring just a month after the WannaCry ransomware attack, NotPetya exploited similar vulnerabilities but with a far more destructive intent. Unlike WannaCry, which primarily aimed to extort money from its victims, NotPetya seemed to be designed for pure destruction, masquerading as ransomware while rendering data irretrievably lost. The attack, which began on June 27, 2017, caused billions of dollars in damages and highlighted the vulnerabilities inherent in global interconnected systems.

NotPetya is named for its similarity to an earlier ransomware strain known as Petya. While Petya encrypted the master boot record (MBR) of infected systems and allowed for the possibility of data recovery upon payment of a ransom, NotPetya took this a step further. It utilized a sophisticated approach that encrypted the file system table, essentially making data recovery impossible even if the ransom was paid. This fundamental difference in operation indicated that NotPetya was not intended as a typical ransomware attack but rather as a cyber weapon aimed at causing maximum disruption and damage.

The attack began in Ukraine, where it quickly spread to affect major organizations, including government agencies, banks, and energy companies. The initial infection vector was a software update mechanism for a popular Ukrainian accounting software called MEDoc. The attackers compromised the MEDoc update server, pushing a malicious update to users of the software. Once downloaded, the update installed the NotPetya malware on victims' systems, initiating the attack. This method of distribution exploited a trusted update channel, making it particularly effective and difficult to detect.

Once installed, NotPetya leveraged multiple techniques to spread across networks, exploiting the same EternalBlue vulnerability in Microsoft's Server Message Block (SMB) protocol that WannaCry had used. However, NotPetya also utilized additional propagation mechanisms, including the EternalRomance exploit and a technique known as credential harvesting, which involved stealing user credentials from infected machines to further propagate the malware. This multifaceted approach enabled NotPetya to spread rapidly and infect a vast number of systems within a short period.

One of the most striking aspects of the NotPetya attack was its ability to affect a wide range of organizations across different sectors and regions. While the initial outbreak was concentrated in Ukraine, the malware quickly spread to numerous countries and industries, affecting some of the world's largest and most prominent companies. Among the high-profile victims were the global shipping giant Maersk, the pharmaceutical company Merck, the food and beverage conglomerate Mondelez, and the advertising firm WPP. The attack also disrupted operations at Rosneft, a major Russian oil company, and impacted several other companies in Europe and the United States.

The scale of disruption caused by NotPetya was unprecedented. Maersk, for instance, had to shut down its IT systems across multiple sites worldwide, leading to significant delays and logistical challenges in its shipping operations. The company later revealed that it had to reinstall 4,000 servers, 45,000 PCs, and 2,500 applications, a monumental task that took several weeks to complete. Merck experienced significant disruptions in its manufacturing processes, which led to a temporary halt in the production of critical medicines and vaccines. Mondelez reported losses due to the interruption of its operations and the need to rebuild its IT infrastructure from scratch. The total financial impact of the attack was estimated to be in the range of $10 billion, making it one of the costliest cyberattacks in history.

The nature of the attack and the entities it affected led many experts to believe that NotPetya was not a traditional ransomware attack but rather an act of cyber warfare. The sophisticated nature of the malware, its rapid spread, and the apparent lack of a genuine mechanism for data recovery indicated that the primary goal was to cause widespread disruption and damage rather than to extort money. This assessment was further supported by the fact that the majority of infections occurred in Ukraine, a country that has been the target of numerous cyberattacks attributed to Russian state actors in the context of ongoing geopolitical tensions.

The attribution of the NotPetya attack has been a subject of extensive investigation and debate. Multiple cybersecurity firms and government agencies have pointed to Russia as the likely origin of the attack. In particular, the U.S., U.K., and several other countries have publicly attributed the attack to the Russian military intelligence agency, GRU. These accusations are based on several factors, including the timing of the attack, the use of malware techniques and tools associated with known Russian cyber operations, and the apparent geopolitical motives behind targeting Ukraine. However, Russia has consistently denied any involvement in the attack.

In the wake of the NotPetya attack, there has been a significant focus on the lessons learned and the implications for cybersecurity practices. One of the key takeaways is the critical importance of securing supply chains and third-party software updates. The initial infection vector for NotPetya was a compromised software update, highlighting the vulnerability of trusted channels and the need for rigorous security measures to protect them. This includes implementing stronger authentication mechanisms, conducting regular security audits of third-party providers, and employing technologies such as code signing to ensure the integrity of software updates.

Another important lesson from the NotPetya attack is the need for robust network segmentation and isolation. The rapid spread of the malware across networks was facilitated by the lack of adequate segmentation, allowing it to propagate freely and infect a large number of systems. Organizations can mitigate the risk of such attacks by implementing network segmentation, which limits the spread of malware and isolates critical systems from the broader network. This approach not only helps to contain the damage but also makes it easier to detect and respond to cyber incidents.

The NotPetya attack also underscored the importance of maintaining up-to-date software and applying security patches in a timely manner. The malware exploited vulnerabilities that had been known and patched by Microsoft several months before the attack. However, many organizations had not applied these patches, leaving their systems vulnerable to exploitation. This highlights the need for organizations to prioritize patch management and ensure that critical updates are deployed promptly across their networks.

In addition to technical measures, the NotPetya attack highlighted the need for comprehensive incident response planning and preparedness. The ability of organizations to quickly detect, respond to, and recover from cyber incidents is crucial in minimizing the impact of such attacks. This includes having an incident response plan in place, conducting regular drills and simulations, and ensuring that all stakeholders are aware of their roles and responsibilities in the event of a cyber incident.

The geopolitical implications of the NotPetya attack are also significant. The attack demonstrated the potential for cyber operations to be used as a tool of statecraft, with the ability to cause significant disruption and damage across borders. This has led to increased calls for international cooperation and the establishment of norms and agreements to prevent and respond to state-sponsored cyber-attacks. The attack also highlighted the need for greater collaboration between the public and private sectors in sharing threat intelligence and coordinating responses to cyber threats.

In terms of policy and regulation, the NotPetya attack has influenced the development of more stringent cybersecurity requirements and standards. For example, the European Union's General Data Protection Regulation (GDPR), which came into effect shortly after the attack, includes provisions that mandate the implementation of appropriate security measures to protect personal data. The attack has also prompted governments and regulatory bodies around the world to introduce new regulations aimed at enhancing the cybersecurity resilience of critical infrastructure and key sectors.

The financial impact of the NotPetya attack has been profound, with losses extending far beyond the immediate costs of system restoration and lost productivity. Many affected companies faced significant financial liabilities due to business interruption, lost revenue, and the costs of rebuilding their IT infrastructure. The attack also led to increased scrutiny from investors, regulators, and customers, highlighting the broader economic risks associated with cyber threats and the importance of robust cybersecurity governance.

Chapter 25: Marriott Data Breach

The Marriott data breach of 2018 stands as one of the largest and most significant data security incidents in history, affecting approximately 500 million guests and revealing critical flaws in data protection and cybersecurity management within large organizations. The breach, which was discovered in September 2018 but had been ongoing since 2014, involved unauthorized access to the Starwood guest reservation database, acquired by Marriott International in 2016. The breach exposed a vast array of sensitive personal information, including names, addresses, phone numbers, email addresses, passport numbers, dates of birth, and, in some cases, encrypted credit card information. This incident not only highlighted the challenges associated with securing large-scale, complex systems but also underscored the long-term risks posed by mergers and acquisitions when integrating disparate IT infrastructures.

The origins of the Marriott breach can be traced back to Starwood Hotels & Resorts Worldwide, which Marriott acquired in a $13.6 billion deal in 2016. Starwood's guest reservation system had been compromised as early as 2014, with hackers gaining unauthorized access to the database and remaining undetected for four years. During this time, they extracted a vast amount of guest information. The breach was only discovered by Marriott on September 8, 2018, when an internal security tool alerted the company to an attempt to access the Starwood guest reservation database. Subsequent investigations revealed that the breach had been ongoing since 2014 and that attackers had been exfiltrating data on a large scale.

The magnitude of the data exposed in the Marriott breach was staggering. According to Marriott's disclosure, the breach affected approximately 500 million guests who had stayed at Starwood properties, including brands such as Sheraton, Westin, and W Hotels. The exposed data included a wide range of personal information, such as names, mailing addresses, phone numbers, email addresses, passport numbers, and Starwood Preferred Guest account information. For approximately 327 million guests, the exposed data included some combination of name, mailing address, phone number, email address, passport number, Starwood Preferred Guest account information, date of birth, gender, arrival and departure information, reservation date, and communication preferences. Additionally, encrypted payment card numbers and expiration dates were exposed for some guests, although Marriott stated that there was no evidence that the encryption keys needed to decrypt this information were compromised.

The breach was a stark reminder of the vulnerabilities inherent in complex, interconnected systems, particularly in the context of mergers and acquisitions. The integration of Starwood's IT systems into Marriott's infrastructure had created significant challenges in terms of data security and management. The breach highlighted the importance of conducting thorough cybersecurity due diligence during mergers and acquisitions to identify and address potential risks associated with integrating different systems and networks.

The response to the breach was swift but underscored the difficulties in managing such a large-scale incident. Marriott launched an investigation with the help of cybersecurity experts and notified law enforcement and regulatory authorities. The company also set up a dedicated website and call center to provide information and assistance to affected guests. Additionally, Marriott offered free enrollment in a personal information monitoring service for one year to those impacted by the breach. Despite these efforts, the company faced significant criticism for the delay in detecting the breach and the initial lack of clarity regarding the scope and impact of the incident.

The Marriott breach had far-reaching implications for both the company and the broader business community. The financial impact on Marriott was significant, with the company facing potential fines, lawsuits, and a loss of consumer trust. The breach also prompted a review of data protection practices across the hospitality industry and other sectors, highlighting the need for more robust cybersecurity measures and the importance of protecting sensitive customer information.

One of the key lessons from the Marriott breach was the importance of effective cybersecurity governance and oversight. The breach revealed weaknesses in Marriott's approach to data security, including inadequate monitoring and detection capabilities. This underscored the need for organizations to invest in comprehensive cybersecurity programs that include regular vulnerability assessments, real-time threat detection, and incident response planning. It also highlighted the importance of maintaining a security-first mindset throughout the organization, from executive leadership to front-line employees.

The breach also brought attention to the challenges associated with securing legacy systems and the integration of IT infrastructures following mergers and acquisitions. The integration of Starwood's systems into Marriott's network had created a complex environment with multiple potential points of vulnerability. This highlighted the need for thorough due diligence and rigorous security assessments during the integration process to identify and mitigate potential risks. It also underscored the importance of maintaining up-to-date systems and ensuring that security patches and updates are applied promptly to protect against known vulnerabilities.

Another significant aspect of the Marriott breach was the exposure of passport numbers and payment card information, which posed serious risks of identity theft and financial fraud for affected guests. The exposure of passport numbers, in particular, raised concerns about the potential misuse of this information for identity theft and other fraudulent activities. This highlighted the need for organizations to implement strong encryption and access controls to protect sensitive personal information and to limit the collection and retention of such data to the minimum necessary for business purposes.

The Marriott breach also had significant regulatory implications, particularly in the context of the European Union's General Data Protection Regulation (GDPR), which had come into effect in May 2018. Under GDPR, organizations are required to implement appropriate technical and organizational measures to protect personal data and are subject to substantial fines for data breaches that result from inadequate security practices. The breach prompted an investigation by the UK's Information Commissioner's Office (ICO), which ultimately proposed a fine of £99.2 million (approximately $124 million) against Marriott for failing to protect customers' personal data. This underscored the importance of compliance with data protection regulations and the potential financial penalties for failing to adequately safeguard personal information.

In addition to financial penalties, the Marriott breach also led to numerous lawsuits, including class-action lawsuits filed by affected guests. These lawsuits sought compensation for damages resulting from the breach, including the costs associated with identity theft and credit monitoring services. The breach also prompted a review of Marriott's data protection practices and policies, leading to increased scrutiny from regulators, investors, and customers.

The breach had a significant impact on Marriott's reputation, with the company facing a loss of consumer trust and confidence. The hospitality industry relies heavily on customer trust, and the breach highlighted the potential reputational damage that can result from a major data security incident. Marriott's response to the breach, including its efforts to provide information and assistance to affected guests, was critical in mitigating the damage to its reputation. However, the incident underscored the importance of maintaining strong data protection practices to build and maintain consumer trust.

In the broader context of cybersecurity, the Marriott breach highlighted the evolving nature of cyber threats and the need for organizations to stay ahead of emerging risks. The breach demonstrated that even large, well-resourced companies are vulnerable to sophisticated cyber-attacks and underscored the importance of maintaining a proactive approach to cybersecurity. This includes investing in advanced threat detection and prevention technologies, conducting regular security assessments and penetration testing, and staying informed about the latest threats and vulnerabilities.

The Marriott breach also underscored the importance of collaboration and information sharing in addressing cyber threats. The breach prompted increased cooperation between the private sector, government agencies, and cybersecurity experts to identify the attackers, understand the methods used, and develop strategies to prevent similar incidents in the future. This highlighted the need for greater collaboration and information sharing to enhance the overall resilience of organizations and critical infrastructure against cyber threats.

Chapter 26: Cambridge Analytica Scandal

The Cambridge Analytica scandal of 2018 represents a watershed moment in the intersection of technology, data privacy, and politics. This scandal not only revealed the vast extent to which personal data can be collected and exploited but also underscored the profound implications such practices can have on democracy and individual privacy. The revelations surrounding Cambridge Analytica's misuse of data from millions of Facebook users highlighted the urgent need for greater transparency, accountability, and regulation in the digital age. The scandal also sparked a global conversation about data privacy, ethics in technology, and the role of social media in shaping public opinion and political outcomes.

The origins of the Cambridge Analytica scandal can be traced back to the data harvesting practices of the now-defunct British political consulting firm, Cambridge Analytica, and its parent company, Strategic Communication Laboratories (SCL). The firm was involved in data analysis and strategic communication for political campaigns, including the 2016 U.S. presidential election and the Brexit referendum in the United Kingdom. The controversy centered around the unauthorized acquisition and use of personal data from approximately 87 million Facebook users, which Cambridge Analytica used to create detailed psychological profiles and target individuals with tailored political advertisements.

The key figure in the scandal was Aleksandr Kogan, a data scientist and researcher at the University of Cambridge. In 2014, Kogan developed a Facebook app called "This Is Your Digital Life," which ostensibly provided users with a personality quiz. While only about 270,000 people directly interacted with the app, it was designed to harvest not only their personal data but also the data of their Facebook friends, thanks to Facebook's then-lenient data-sharing policies. This allowed Kogan to collect data on millions of users, including information such as likes, interests, and demographic details.

Kogan's app collected this data under the guise of academic research, but he later sold the data to Cambridge Analytica, violating Facebook's policies and the terms of consent given by the users. Cambridge Analytica then used this data to create psychographic profiles, which are detailed representations of individuals' personality traits, preferences, and behaviors. These profiles were used to deliver highly personalized political messages aimed at influencing voters' opinions and behaviors.

The scandal came to light in March 2018, when whistleblower Christopher Wylie, a former Cambridge Analytica employee, revealed the company's practices to The Guardian and The New York Times. Wylie described how Cambridge Analytica had used the data to target voters with manipulative and sometimes misleading political advertisements during the 2016 U.S. presidential election, where the firm worked on behalf of the Trump campaign. He also detailed the company's involvement in other political campaigns, including the Brexit referendum.

The impact of the scandal was immediate and far-reaching. Facebook faced intense scrutiny from the media, regulators, and the public for its role in allowing the data to be harvested and for its failure to protect users' privacy. In April 2018, Facebook CEO Mark Zuckerberg testified before the U.S. Congress, acknowledging the company's responsibility in the breach and pledging to improve data security and privacy practices. Facebook also faced legal action from multiple entities, including the U.S. Federal Trade Commission (FTC), which imposed a $5 billion fine on the company for privacy violations in 2019, the largest fine ever imposed by the FTC at that time.

The scandal also had significant political ramifications. The misuse of data by Cambridge Analytica highlighted the potential for data-driven manipulation in democratic processes, raising concerns about the integrity of elections and the influence of foreign actors. The revelations fueled debates about the need for stronger regulations to protect data privacy and the role of social media platforms in political campaigns. In the UK, the Information Commissioner's Office (ICO) launched an investigation into the misuse of data by Cambridge Analytica, which ultimately led to the company declaring bankruptcy in May 2018.

The Cambridge Analytica scandal also brought to light broader issues related to the collection and use of personal data by technology companies. It underscored the asymmetry of power between users and companies that collect and control vast amounts of data, highlighting the lack of transparency and accountability in how data is collected, shared, and used. This sparked a global movement for greater data protection and privacy rights, leading to the introduction and strengthening of data protection laws in many countries, including the European Union's General Data Protection Regulation (GDPR) and the California Consumer Privacy Act (CCPA).

In addition to regulatory changes, the scandal prompted significant changes in corporate practices. Companies across the tech industry were compelled to reevaluate their data practices, implement stronger privacy protections, and improve transparency in their dealings with users. For Facebook, this meant overhauling its data privacy policies, restricting third-party access to data, and enhancing user control over personal information. The company also launched a series of initiatives to address misinformation and improve the security of its platform.

The Cambridge Analytica scandal also had a profound impact on public awareness and attitudes toward data privacy. It highlighted the extent to which personal data can be collected and used without individuals' knowledge or consent, leading to a growing awareness of the importance of protecting personal information and the risks associated with data sharing. This has fueled a broader cultural shift towards greater skepticism of technology companies and a demand for more ethical practices in the handling of personal data.

The scandal also raised important ethical questions about the use of data in political campaigns and the responsibility of technology companies in ensuring the integrity of democratic processes. It underscored the potential for data-driven manipulation and the need for ethical guidelines and regulations to govern the use of data in politics. This has led to increased calls for transparency in political advertising, including the disclosure of funding sources and the targeting criteria used in digital campaigns.

In the academic and research community, the scandal prompted a reevaluation of the ethical standards for conducting research involving personal data. It highlighted the need for stricter oversight and ethical guidelines to ensure that research practices respect individuals' privacy and consent. This has led to the development of new frameworks and best practices for data ethics, including the responsible use of data and the protection of individual rights in research and technology development.

The Cambridge Analytica scandal also had a lasting impact on the landscape of digital advertising and data-driven marketing. It highlighted the potential for abuse in the collection and use of personal data for targeted advertising and underscored the need for greater transparency and accountability in the digital advertising ecosystem. This has led to increased scrutiny of data brokers and third-party data providers, as well as efforts to improve the transparency and accountability of data collection and use in digital advertising.

In the political sphere, the scandal underscored the importance of safeguarding the integrity of elections and protecting democratic processes from manipulation and interference. It highlighted the potential for digital platforms to be used as tools for political influence and manipulation, raising concerns about the role of technology in shaping public opinion and political outcomes. This has led to increased efforts to secure electoral processes, including measures to combat misinformation, enhance the security of voting systems, and protect the integrity of political campaigns.

The scandal also highlighted the need for international cooperation in addressing data privacy and cybersecurity challenges. The global nature of the Cambridge Analytica scandal underscored the interconnectedness of digital platforms and the need for coordinated efforts to address data privacy and security issues across borders. This has led to increased collaboration between governments, regulatory bodies, and international organizations to develop frameworks and standards for data protection and privacy on a global scale.

In the aftermath of the scandal, Cambridge Analytica ceased operations, and its parent company, SCL, also shut down. The closure of the company marked the end of one of the most controversial and influential political consulting firms in recent history, but the legacy of the scandal continues to shape the discourse around data privacy, ethics, and the role of technology in society. The lessons learned from the Cambridge Analytica scandal continue to inform efforts to protect personal data, ensure the integrity of democratic processes, and promote ethical practices in the use of technology and data.

Chapter 27: Magecart Attacks

Magecart attacks, occurring prominently between 2018 and 2019, represent a series of highly sophisticated and damaging cyberattacks that targeted e-commerce websites and online payment platforms. These attacks were primarily aimed at stealing sensitive financial information, such as credit card details and personal data, from unsuspecting consumers making purchases online. Magecart refers to a collection of cybercriminal groups that used various techniques to infiltrate and exploit vulnerabilities in websites, often inserting malicious scripts to skim payment data during transactions. The widespread and impactful nature of these attacks underscored significant weaknesses in web security and prompted a reevaluation of cybersecurity practices across the e-commerce industry.

The term "Magecart" is derived from the initial focus of these attacks on websites using the Magento e-commerce platform. However, the scope of Magecart operations quickly expanded to include a variety of platforms and content management systems. The attackers employed a technique known as "web skimming" or "formjacking," where they injected malicious JavaScript code into websites' checkout pages. This code would then capture sensitive information entered by customers, such as credit card numbers, names, addresses, and other personal details, and transmit it to the attackers' servers.

The modus operandi of Magecart attacks involved several stages. Initially, the attackers identified vulnerable websites by scanning for known security flaws in e-commerce platforms, third-party plugins, or content management systems. They exploited these vulnerabilities to gain unauthorized access to the websites' servers. Once inside, the attackers typically inserted their malicious code into the payment processing pages. This code was designed to be unobtrusive and difficult to detect, often mimicking legitimate scripts used by the websites. The malicious code would activate when a customer entered their payment details, capturing the data and sending it to the attackers in real time.

One of the most significant aspects of Magecart attacks was the use of third-party dependencies and supply chain weaknesses to infiltrate websites. Many e-commerce sites rely on third-party services for functions such as analytics, advertising, and payment processing. Magecart attackers often targeted these third-party services to compromise multiple websites simultaneously. By infiltrating a third-party service provider, the attackers could inject their malicious code into all websites that used the compromised service, exponentially increasing the reach and impact of their attacks. This supply chain attack vector made it difficult for individual websites to protect themselves, as the security of their own site depended on the security of multiple external services.

The scale and impact of Magecart attacks were immense, affecting some of the world's largest and most well-known brands. One of the most notable incidents occurred in June 2018, when British Airways suffered a breach that resulted in the theft of approximately 380,000 payment card details. The attackers injected malicious code into the airline's website and mobile app, capturing payment information as customers made bookings. The breach was significant not only for the volume of data stolen but also because it demonstrated the capability of Magecart attackers to compromise high-profile targets.

Another major incident involved Ticketmaster, a leading ticket sales and distribution company. In 2018, Magecart attackers compromised a third-party service used by Ticketmaster, allowing them to inject malicious code into the payment pages of the company's website. The breach affected tens of thousands of customers, exposing their payment card details and personal information. The attack on Ticketmaster highlighted the vulnerability of large enterprises that rely on third-party services, emphasizing the need for comprehensive security measures that extend beyond the immediate boundaries of the organization.

Magecart attacks also targeted numerous other high-profile companies, including Newegg, an online retailer specializing in computer hardware and consumer electronics, and the hotel chain Marriott International. In the case of Newegg, attackers injected malicious code into the company's payment page, capturing credit card details from customers making purchases. Similarly, the attack on Marriott involved the compromise of a third-party service provider, resulting in the theft of payment card information from thousands of customers.

The widespread nature of Magecart attacks had significant implications for both consumers and businesses. For consumers, the theft of payment card details and personal information posed serious risks of financial fraud and identity theft. Victims often faced substantial financial losses and the inconvenience of having to cancel and replace compromised cards. For businesses, the attacks resulted in significant financial losses, damage to reputation, and potential legal liabilities. Companies affected by Magecart attacks faced the costs of investigating and remediating the breaches, as well as potential fines and penalties from regulatory bodies.

The response to Magecart attacks involved a combination of technical measures, regulatory actions, and increased awareness and education. Businesses were urged to adopt more stringent security practices, including regular vulnerability assessments, real-time monitoring for suspicious activity, and the implementation of secure coding practices. The use of Content Security Policies (CSP) was recommended to help prevent unauthorized code from being executed on websites. CSPs allow website administrators to specify which sources of content are considered safe, thereby blocking any attempts to inject malicious code from unauthorized sources.

Regulatory bodies also took action in response to Magecart attacks, emphasizing the importance of compliance with data protection and cybersecurity regulations. For example, the European Union's General Data Protection Regulation (GDPR) requires companies to implement appropriate technical and organizational measures to protect personal data and to report data breaches to regulators and affected individuals within 72 hours of discovery. Companies that fail to comply with these requirements can face substantial fines and penalties. The enforcement of GDPR and similar regulations in other jurisdictions highlighted the need for businesses to prioritize data protection and cybersecurity as part of their overall risk management strategy.

The Magecart attacks also underscored the importance of collaboration and information sharing in the fight against cybercrime. Law enforcement agencies, cybersecurity firms, and industry groups worked together to investigate the attacks, share threat intelligence, and develop strategies to mitigate the risks associated with web skimming and formjacking. This collaborative approach helped to improve the overall resilience of the e-commerce industry against similar threats.

In addition to technical and regulatory measures, there was a significant emphasis on raising awareness and educating both businesses and consumers about the risks associated with Magecart attacks. Businesses were encouraged to implement best practices for securing their websites and payment systems, including regular security audits, employee training, and the use of secure development frameworks. Consumers were advised to be vigilant when making online purchases, to use secure payment methods, and to monitor their financial accounts for signs of unauthorized activity.

The Magecart attacks also highlighted the need for ongoing innovation and investment in cybersecurity technologies. The use of advanced threat detection and prevention tools, such as machine learning-based anomaly detection and automated threat intelligence platforms, was recommended to help identify and respond to potential threats in real time. The development of new technologies and approaches to secure online transactions, such as tokenization and end-to-end encryption, also played a critical role in enhancing the security of e-commerce platforms and protecting sensitive payment data.

In the aftermath of the Magecart attacks, there was a renewed focus on the importance of securing the digital supply chain. Businesses were encouraged to conduct thorough due diligence when selecting third-party service providers, to establish clear security requirements and expectations, and to continuously monitor the security posture of their supply chain partners. This approach helped to reduce the risk of supply chain attacks and to ensure that all parties involved in the processing of payment data adhered to the highest standards of cybersecurity.

The impact of the Magecart attacks extended beyond the immediate financial and reputational damage to affected businesses. The attacks prompted a broader reevaluation of the role of cybersecurity in the digital economy, highlighting the need for a more comprehensive and proactive approach to managing cyber risks. This included the recognition that cybersecurity is not just a technical issue but a critical business function that requires the involvement and commitment of senior leadership, clear governance structures, and a culture of security awareness throughout the organization.

The lessons learned from the Magecart attacks continue to inform and shape the cybersecurity landscape, driving efforts to improve the security of e-commerce platforms and to protect consumers from the risks of online fraud and identity theft. The attacks highlighted the importance of adopting a multi-layered approach to cybersecurity, combining technical measures, regulatory compliance, and a strong focus on education and awareness. This holistic approach helps to build resilience against the evolving threat landscape and to ensure that businesses and consumers can continue to engage in online transactions with confidence and security.

Chapter 28: Capital One Data Breach

The Capital One data breach of 2019 is a significant event in the landscape of cybersecurity, highlighting the vulnerabilities of cloud computing services and the critical importance of robust security measures to protect sensitive data. This breach, which exposed the personal and financial information of over 100 million individuals in the United States and Canada, serves as a stark reminder of the challenges faced by organizations in safeguarding their data against increasingly sophisticated cyber threats. The incident not only had profound implications for Capital One but also for the broader financial services industry and the regulatory environment surrounding data protection.

The breach was orchestrated by Paige A. Thompson, a former Amazon Web Services (AWS) employee, who exploited a misconfigured firewall to gain unauthorized access to Capital One's data stored on AWS's cloud infrastructure. The attack, which took place between March 12 and July 17, 2019, exposed a wide range of sensitive information, including names, addresses, phone numbers, email addresses, dates of birth, Social Security numbers, and financial data such as credit scores, credit limits, balances, and transaction history. The breach also exposed information related to approximately 140,000 Social Security numbers and 80,000 linked bank account numbers from credit card customers.

Thompson's background as a former AWS employee gave her the technical knowledge and expertise needed to exploit the misconfiguration in Capital One's cloud environment. She used a technique known as "server-side request forgery" (SSRF), which involves manipulating a server into making unauthorized requests on behalf of the attacker. This allowed her to bypass the security controls that were intended to protect Capital One's data and to gain access to the sensitive information stored in the cloud.

One of the key factors that contributed to the breach was the misconfiguration of a Web Application Firewall (WAF) that was designed to protect Capital One's web applications from malicious traffic. The WAF was intended to filter and monitor HTTP requests to and from the web application, blocking any potentially harmful requests. However, due to an error in the configuration, the WAF was left vulnerable to SSRF attacks, allowing Thompson to exploit the weakness and gain access to the data stored on AWS.

The breach also highlighted the importance of proper access control and monitoring in cloud environments. Despite the sophisticated security measures implemented by AWS, the responsibility for securing data in the cloud ultimately lies with the customer, in this case, Capital One. The breach revealed weaknesses in Capital One's security practices, including inadequate monitoring and detection capabilities, which allowed the attacker to remain undetected for an extended period.

The impact of the breach was significant and far-reaching. For the affected individuals, the exposure of personal and financial information posed serious risks of identity theft and financial fraud. Victims faced the potential for unauthorized use of their credit card information, fraudulent account openings, and other forms of financial exploitation. The breach also had a substantial impact on Capital One, resulting in significant financial losses, damage to the company's reputation, and potential legal liabilities.

In response to the breach, Capital One took several measures to mitigate the impact and to strengthen its security posture. The company notified affected individuals and offered free credit monitoring and identity protection services. Capital One also launched an internal investigation to determine the cause of the breach and to identify any additional vulnerabilities in its systems. The company worked closely with law enforcement agencies, including the

FBI, which ultimately led to the arrest and prosecution of Paige A. Thompson.

The Capital One breach also prompted increased scrutiny from regulatory bodies. The Office of the Comptroller of the Currency (OCC), the U.S. Treasury Department's regulatory body overseeing national banks, issued a $80 million fine against Capital One in August 2020. The fine was imposed for the bank's failure to establish effective risk assessment processes and internal controls before migrating its IT operations to the cloud. The OCC's action underscored the importance of regulatory compliance and the need for financial institutions to implement robust security measures to protect sensitive data.

The breach had broader implications for the financial services industry and the use of cloud computing. The incident highlighted the risks associated with migrating critical IT infrastructure to the cloud and underscored the need for organizations to adopt a comprehensive approach to cloud security. This includes conducting thorough risk assessments, implementing strong access controls, continuously monitoring for threats, and ensuring that security configurations are regularly reviewed and updated.

The breach also led to increased calls for stronger data protection regulations and enhanced enforcement of existing laws. In the United States, the incident prompted discussions about the need for a federal data privacy law that would establish consistent standards for data protection and security across all states. The breach also reinforced the importance of international cooperation in addressing data breaches and protecting individuals' personal information in an increasingly interconnected world.

The Capital One breach also served as a catalyst for improvements in cloud security practices and technologies. Organizations were encouraged to adopt best practices for securing cloud environments, including the use of encryption to protect sensitive data, the implementation of multi-factor authentication for accessing cloud services, and the deployment of advanced threat detection and response tools. The incident also highlighted the importance of third-party security assessments and audits to identify and address potential vulnerabilities in cloud infrastructure.

In the aftermath of the breach, there was a significant emphasis on the need for a cultural shift in the approach to cybersecurity within organizations. This included the recognition that cybersecurity is not just a technical issue but a critical business function that requires the involvement and commitment of senior leadership. Organizations were encouraged to foster a culture of security awareness, where employees at all levels understand the importance of protecting sensitive data and are equipped with the knowledge and tools to identify and respond to potential threats.

The breach also highlighted the importance of transparency and communication in the event of a data breach. Capital One's response to the incident included timely notification of affected individuals and clear communication about the steps being taken to mitigate the impact of the breach. This approach helped to build trust with customers and stakeholders and to demonstrate the company's commitment to addressing the issue and preventing future breaches.

The lessons learned from the Capital One breach continue to inform the approach to cybersecurity and data protection in the financial services industry and beyond. The incident underscored the importance of a multi-layered approach to security, combining technical measures, regulatory compliance, and a strong focus on education and awareness. It also highlighted the need for organizations to continuously evolve their security practices in response to emerging threats and to adopt a proactive approach to managing cyber risks.

Chapter 29: Desjardins Data Breach

The Desjardins data breach of 2019 stands as one of the most significant and far-reaching cybersecurity incidents in Canadian history, affecting nearly 4.2 million individuals and 173,000 businesses. This breach not only exposed sensitive personal and financial information but also underscored critical vulnerabilities in data security practices, particularly within financial institutions. The breach's ramifications extended beyond immediate financial loss, prompting widespread scrutiny, regulatory action, and a profound reevaluation of data protection measures across the industry. The Desjardins case serves as a stark reminder of the necessity for robust data security protocols and highlights the complexities and challenges involved in safeguarding sensitive information.

Desjardins Group, a prominent financial cooperative based in Quebec, Canada, was the target of an extensive internal data theft that came to light in June 2019. Unlike many other high-profile data breaches that result from external cyberattacks, the Desjardins breach was perpetrated by an insider—an employee with legitimate access to sensitive data. The breach exposed personal information including names, addresses, birthdates, social insurance numbers, email addresses, and detailed financial information such as transaction histories and credit data.

The perpetrator, later identified as an employee in Desjardins' administrative services, exploited their position to systematically collect and exfiltrate data over a period of several months, possibly even years. The individual used their access to internal systems to gather the data, which was then transferred to unauthorized external parties. This insider threat scenario highlights a critical risk faced by organizations: the potential for trusted employees to misuse their access to data for malicious purposes. The breach was eventually discovered when suspicious transactions were reported to law enforcement, leading to an internal investigation by Desjardins.

The scale of the breach was staggering, affecting approximately 2.9 million individual members and 173,000 business clients. The exposed data included not just basic personal information but also highly sensitive financial details that could be used for identity theft, financial fraud, and other malicious activities. The exposure of social insurance numbers was particularly concerning, as this information can be used to commit various forms of identity theft, including opening new credit accounts, filing fraudulent tax returns, and accessing government benefits.

In the wake of the breach, Desjardins faced significant challenges in managing the fallout and addressing the concerns of its members and clients. The organization took immediate steps to mitigate the impact, including offering free credit monitoring services, enhancing security measures, and cooperating fully with law enforcement and regulatory authorities. Desjardins also initiated a comprehensive review of its internal security practices and implemented additional safeguards to prevent similar incidents in the future.

The breach had far-reaching implications for the affected individuals and businesses. Many faced the daunting task of monitoring their financial accounts for signs of fraud, placing alerts on their credit reports, and taking additional steps to protect their identities. The psychological impact of the breach was also significant, as victims grappled with the uncertainty and anxiety of potential identity theft and financial fraud. The breach also eroded trust in Desjardins, with many members questioning the organization's ability to protect their sensitive information and considering alternative financial service providers.

From a regulatory perspective, the breach underscored the need for stronger data protection laws and more robust oversight of financial institutions. In response to the incident, Canadian regulators launched investigations into the breach and assessed Desjardins' compliance with existing data protection regulations. The breach also prompted calls for legislative reforms to enhance data security requirements and to increase penalties for organizations that fail to protect personal information adequately.

The breach highlighted several key areas where improvements were needed, both within Desjardins and across the broader financial services industry. One of the primary issues was the need for better access control and monitoring. The perpetrator of the breach was able to exploit their legitimate access to data without detection for an extended period, underscoring the importance of implementing robust access controls and continuous monitoring to detect and respond to suspicious activity in real time.

Another critical area for improvement was the need for enhanced data security training and awareness programs for employees. The breach demonstrated that even trusted employees can pose significant risks if they misuse their access to sensitive data. Organizations need to ensure that all employees understand their responsibilities for protecting data and are aware of the potential consequences of data breaches. This includes providing regular training on data security best practices, the importance of data privacy, and the risks associated with insider threats.

The breach also highlighted the importance of implementing comprehensive data protection measures, including encryption, data masking, and data minimization. Encrypting sensitive data both at rest and in transit can help protect it from unauthorized access, even if it is exfiltrated. Data masking can be used to obscure sensitive information in a way that preserves its usefulness for legitimate purposes while protecting it from misuse. Data minimization involves collecting only the data that is necessary for specific purposes and retaining it only for as long as necessary, reducing the potential impact of data breaches.

The Desjardins breach also underscored the need for organizations to have robust incident response plans in place. A well-prepared incident response plan can help organizations quickly identify and contain breaches, mitigate their impact, and communicate effectively with stakeholders. This includes having a clear process for reporting breaches, coordinating with law enforcement and regulatory authorities, and providing timely and transparent communication to affected individuals and the public.

In the aftermath of the breach, Desjardins took several steps to enhance its data security practices and to rebuild trust with its members and clients. The organization implemented new security technologies, including advanced threat detection and response tools, and strengthened its access control policies to limit employees' access to sensitive data based on their roles and responsibilities. Desjardins also established a dedicated cybersecurity team to oversee its data protection efforts and to ensure that it remains compliant with regulatory requirements.

The breach also led to increased collaboration between financial institutions and government agencies to address cybersecurity threats and to improve the overall security of the financial sector. This included sharing threat intelligence, developing best practices for data protection, and participating in industry-wide initiatives to enhance cybersecurity resilience. The breach served as a catalyst for greater cooperation and coordination in the fight against cybercrime and highlighted the need for a collective approach to safeguarding sensitive information.

The Desjardins breach also had broader implications for the financial services industry and for data protection practices globally. The incident highlighted the growing threat of insider attacks and the importance of implementing comprehensive security measures to protect against both external and internal threats. It also underscored the need for organizations to take a proactive approach to data protection, including regular security assessments, continuous monitoring, and the adoption of best practices for data security.

The breach prompted a reexamination of data protection laws and regulations, both in Canada and internationally. In Canada, the incident led to calls for stronger data protection legislation and increased penalties for organizations that fail to protect personal information adequately. It also prompted a broader discussion about the need for a federal data privacy law that would establish consistent standards for data protection across all provinces and territories.

Internationally, the breach highlighted the importance of global cooperation in addressing data protection challenges and the need for harmonized data protection regulations. The incident underscored the interconnected nature of the global financial system and the importance of ensuring that data protection practices are consistent and effective across borders. This includes the need for international agreements and frameworks to facilitate cooperation and information sharing in the event of data breaches and other cybersecurity incidents.

The Desjardins breach also served as a wake-up call for organizations in other sectors, highlighting the importance of robust data protection measures and the need to take cybersecurity threats seriously. The incident demonstrated that no organization is immune to data breaches and that the consequences of failing to protect sensitive information can be severe. It also highlighted the need for organizations to prioritize data protection as a key component of their overall risk management strategy and to invest in the technologies, processes, and people needed to safeguard their data.

Chapter 30: SolarWinds Hack

The SolarWinds hack of 2020 stands as one of the most complex and far-reaching cyber espionage campaigns in modern history. This incident not only highlighted the vulnerabilities inherent in the global software supply chain but also underscored the sophistication and persistence of state-sponsored cyber operations. The hack, attributed to a group associated with Russian intelligence, involved the infiltration of SolarWinds, a major IT management software provider, leading to the compromise of thousands of organizations, including prominent U.S. government agencies and Fortune 500 companies. The scale, depth, and implications of the SolarWinds hack have profound ramifications for cybersecurity, international relations, and national security.

The attack began as early as March 2020, when malicious actors managed to gain access to the internal systems of SolarWinds. The attackers targeted the company's Orion software, a popular network management tool used by a vast array of organizations worldwide. By compromising SolarWinds' software development environment, the attackers were able to inject a sophisticated backdoor, later dubbed "SUNBURST," into updates of the Orion platform. This backdoor was then distributed to an estimated 18,000 customers who downloaded and installed the tainted updates, unwittingly providing the attackers with a stealthy entry point into their networks.

The sophistication of the attack was evident in its meticulous planning and execution. The SUNBURST backdoor was designed to be highly covert, employing advanced techniques to avoid detection by traditional security measures. Once installed, the backdoor laid dormant for up to two weeks before initiating communication with command-and-control servers operated by the attackers. This delay helped to avoid raising suspicions and allowed the attackers to establish a foothold in the compromised networks. The backdoor then executed commands to retrieve further payloads and establish persistent access, enabling the attackers to exfiltrate data and potentially deploy additional malware.

The use of a supply chain attack as the vector for the breach highlighted a critical vulnerability in the cybersecurity landscape. By targeting SolarWinds, the attackers were able to bypass the security defenses of multiple high-profile organizations simultaneously. This type of attack is particularly challenging to defend against because it exploits trusted relationships between software vendors and their customers. Organizations typically assume that updates from a reputable vendor are safe, and this trust was leveraged by the attackers to distribute their malicious code widely and surreptitiously.

The impact of the SolarWinds hack was unprecedented in its scope and scale. Among the affected entities were numerous U.S. federal agencies, including the Departments of Homeland Security, State, and Treasury, as well as critical infrastructure providers, technology companies, and academic institutions. The attackers gained access to sensitive information, including internal communications, classified documents, and proprietary data. The full extent of the data exfiltrated during the attack remains unclear, but it is widely believed to include highly sensitive and potentially classified information.

One of the most concerning aspects of the SolarWinds hack was the potential for long-term damage. The attackers were able to maintain persistent access to compromised networks for months before the breach was discovered. This prolonged access provided ample opportunity to gather intelligence, plant additional backdoors, and potentially sabotage critical systems. The risk of future exploitation remains a significant concern, as it is challenging to fully remove all traces of the attackers' presence from compromised networks.

The discovery of the breach in December 2020 was made by cybersecurity firm FireEye, which itself became a victim of the attack. FireEye's investigation into an unusual incident involving the theft of its red team tools led to the identification of the SUNBURST backdoor and the realization that the attack was part of a broader campaign affecting multiple organizations. The disclosure of the breach prompted a flurry of activity from affected organizations to assess the damage, mitigate the threat, and enhance their security measures to prevent further intrusions.

The response to the SolarWinds hack involved a coordinated effort from government agencies, private sector companies, and cybersecurity experts. The U.S. government took several actions to address the breach, including issuing emergency directives to federal agencies to disconnect affected systems, conducting forensic investigations, and implementing measures to enhance the security of critical infrastructure. The Biden administration also imposed sanctions on Russia in response to the attack, signaling the seriousness of the breach and the determination to hold the perpetrators accountable.

The SolarWinds hack also prompted significant changes in cybersecurity practices and policies. Organizations across the globe reevaluated their security measures, with a particular focus on improving supply chain security, enhancing monitoring and detection capabilities, and adopting a zero-trust security model. The concept of zero trust, which assumes that all network traffic is potentially malicious and requires continuous verification, gained renewed attention as a means to mitigate the risk of future supply chain attacks.

The breach also highlighted the importance of threat intelligence and information sharing in the fight against cyber threats. The collaborative efforts of cybersecurity firms, government agencies, and affected organizations were critical in identifying the scope of the attack, sharing indicators of compromise, and developing strategies to mitigate the threat. This incident underscored the need for robust mechanisms to facilitate the rapid exchange of threat intelligence and to coordinate responses to large-scale cyber incidents.

From a policy perspective, the SolarWinds hack spurred discussions about the need for stronger regulations and standards to enhance the security of software supply chains. There were calls for increased oversight of software vendors, including requirements for regular security audits, vulnerability assessments, and the implementation of secure software development practices. The breach also highlighted the need for greater accountability and transparency in the cybersecurity practices of software providers, with an emphasis on ensuring that they adhere to best practices for securing their development environments and protecting their customers' data.

The SolarWinds hack also had significant implications for international relations and national security. The breach was widely attributed to a state-sponsored group associated with Russian intelligence, and it was seen as part of a broader strategy of cyber espionage and disruption. The attack underscored the growing threat posed by state-sponsored cyber activities and highlighted the need for a coordinated international response to address these challenges. The incident also prompted discussions about the need for norms and agreements to govern state behavior in cyberspace and to reduce the risk of escalation and conflict resulting from cyber operations.

In the aftermath of the SolarWinds hack, there was a renewed emphasis on the importance of cybersecurity resilience and the need to prepare for and respond to cyber incidents. Organizations were encouraged to develop comprehensive incident response plans, conduct regular cybersecurity drills, and invest in technologies and processes to enhance their ability to detect and respond to cyber threats. The breach also highlighted the importance of building a culture of cybersecurity within organizations, where employees at all levels are aware of the risks and take an active role in protecting their networks and data.

The SolarWinds hack also served as a wake-up call for the broader technology industry, prompting a reevaluation of the security practices of software vendors and cloud service providers. The incident underscored the critical role that these entities play in the cybersecurity ecosystem and the need for them to adopt rigorous security measures to protect their customers and their own infrastructure. There were calls for increased investment in cybersecurity research and development, as well as for greater collaboration between the public and private sectors to address the evolving threat landscape.

Chapter 31: Twitter Bitcoin Scam

The Twitter Bitcoin scam of 2020, also known as the "Twitter hack," is a striking example of the potential vulnerabilities of social media platforms and the profound implications of such breaches on a global scale. This unprecedented attack, executed on July 15, 2020, involved the compromise of numerous high-profile Twitter accounts and the subsequent orchestration of a large-scale cryptocurrency scam. The incident not only exposed significant weaknesses in Twitter's security protocols but also highlighted the broader risks associated with social media and the growing menace of cybercrime. The attack's ramifications extended far beyond the immediate financial impact, raising serious concerns about the security of digital communications and the potential for malicious actors to exploit social media platforms for various nefarious purposes.

The Twitter Bitcoin scam began when a group of hackers successfully gained access to Twitter's internal systems. This access was reportedly achieved through a combination of social engineering techniques and the exploitation of weak security practices among Twitter employees. The attackers targeted a handful of Twitter employees with access to internal tools and coerced them into providing credentials. This initial access allowed the hackers to bypass Twitter's security controls and gain administrative access to high-profile accounts.

Once inside Twitter's system, the attackers used their privileged access to hijack the accounts of numerous prominent individuals and organizations. Among the compromised accounts were those of former U.S. President Barack Obama, Tesla CEO Elon Musk, Microsoft co-founder Bill Gates, Amazon CEO Jeff Bezos, and numerous others, including corporate accounts like Apple and Uber. The attackers also took over cryptocurrency-related accounts, such as those of Binance and Coinbase, adding a veneer of legitimacy to their scam.

The hackers posted a series of tweets from these high-profile accounts, promoting a Bitcoin giveaway scam. The tweets typically included messages promising to double any Bitcoin sent to a specified address, as a gesture of goodwill or charity. For instance, from Elon Musk's account, a tweet read, "I'm feeling generous because of COVID-19. I'll double any BTC payment sent to my BTC address for the next hour. Good luck, and stay safe out there!" Similar messages were posted from other compromised accounts, creating a sense of urgency and trustworthiness due to the reputations of the individuals and entities involved.

The coordinated timing and execution of the tweets created a sense of legitimacy and urgency, leading many unsuspecting followers to fall victim to the scam. The attackers managed to collect over $100,000 worth of Bitcoin in just a few hours before the scheme was detected and the tweets were removed. The funds were transferred to several Bitcoin wallets, making it challenging to trace the transactions and identify the perpetrators.

The immediate response to the breach was swift but chaotic. Twitter quickly locked down the affected accounts to prevent further unauthorized tweets and temporarily restricted the ability of verified users to tweet altogether. The company also launched an internal investigation to determine how the breach occurred and to assess the extent of the damage. In the following days, Twitter provided updates on its findings and the steps being taken to secure its platform and prevent similar incidents in the future.

The fallout from the Twitter Bitcoin scam was significant, both for Twitter and the broader community. The breach highlighted glaring security vulnerabilities within Twitter's internal systems and the susceptibility of social media platforms to sophisticated cyberattacks. The incident raised serious concerns about the potential misuse of social media for disinformation, financial fraud, and other malicious activities. It also underscored the need for stronger security measures, particularly for high-profile and influential accounts that could be targets for cybercriminals.

The implications of the breach extended beyond financial loss. The compromise of high-profile accounts underscored the potential for social media to be used as a tool for manipulation and disruption. The attack demonstrated how malicious actors could exploit the trust and reach of influential figures to propagate scams, spread misinformation, and potentially sow discord. This was especially concerning given the timing of the attack, amid the global COVID-19 pandemic and the lead-up to the U.S. presidential election, periods of heightened vulnerability and public uncertainty.

In response to the breach, Twitter implemented several immediate security enhancements. The company increased the complexity of internal security protocols, requiring additional verification for account access and implementing more robust monitoring of suspicious activities. Twitter also announced plans to conduct a comprehensive review of its security practices and to invest in longer-term improvements to safeguard its platform against future attacks.

The incident prompted a broader discussion about the security of social media platforms and the responsibilities of technology companies in protecting user data and preventing abuse. There were calls for stricter regulations and oversight to ensure that social media companies implement adequate security measures and are held accountable for breaches. The incident also highlighted the need for greater transparency from social media companies regarding their security practices and the steps they take to protect users from cyber threats.

The Twitter Bitcoin scam also had legal and regulatory repercussions. U.S. lawmakers called for investigations into the breach and for hearings to discuss the implications for cybersecurity and social media regulation. The Federal Bureau of Investigation (FBI) and other law enforcement agencies launched investigations into the attack, seeking to identify and apprehend the perpetrators. The incident underscored the importance of robust legal frameworks to address cybercrime and to hold responsible parties accountable for breaches.

In the aftermath of the breach, several individuals were arrested and charged in connection with the attack. Among them was Graham Ivan Clark, a 17-year-old from Florida, who was identified as the mastermind behind the scheme. Clark and his accomplices were charged with multiple counts of fraud and hacking-related offenses, and they faced significant legal consequences for their actions. The arrests highlighted the challenges of tracing and prosecuting cybercriminals, particularly those who operate across jurisdictions and use sophisticated methods to conceal their identities and activities.

The Twitter Bitcoin scam also highlighted the critical role of user awareness in preventing cyber fraud. The success of the scam was partly due to the trust that users placed in the compromised accounts and the urgency of the messages posted by the attackers. The incident underscored the importance of educating users about the risks of online scams and the need to exercise caution when dealing with unsolicited offers and requests for financial transactions, even when they appear to come from trusted sources.

The breach also spurred discussions about the security practices of cryptocurrency platforms and the vulnerabilities associated with digital currencies. The use of Bitcoin in the scam highlighted the challenges of tracing and recovering funds in the cryptocurrency ecosystem, where transactions are often anonymous and irreversible. This incident underscored the need for stronger security measures and regulatory oversight to protect users and to prevent the misuse of cryptocurrencies for illegal activities.

Chapter 32: Blackbaud Ransomware Attack

The Blackbaud ransomware attack of 2020 stands as a stark example of the vulnerabilities that large-scale data management systems face in the realm of cybersecurity. This incident not only highlighted the growing menace of ransomware as a cyber threat but also underscored the far-reaching consequences of data breaches for organizations that rely heavily on external vendors for managing sensitive information. The attack, which compromised the data of numerous non-profits, educational institutions, and healthcare organizations, revealed significant weaknesses in Blackbaud's security measures and prompted a comprehensive reevaluation of data protection practices across the industry. The Blackbaud attack offers a detailed case study in the complexities and ramifications of modern cybercrime, illustrating the need for robust cybersecurity frameworks and vigilant data management practices.

Blackbaud, a prominent provider of cloud-based software and services tailored for non-profit organizations, educational institutions, and other entities, was targeted in a sophisticated ransomware attack that came to light in July 2020. The company provides a range of services, including fundraising, financial management, and donor relationship management, and serves a broad clientele globally. The attack, which initially occurred in May 2020, involved cybercriminals gaining unauthorized access to Blackbaud's systems and deploying ransomware to encrypt data. The attackers then demanded a ransom payment in exchange for a decryption key and the assurance that stolen data would not be publicly released.

The breach's discovery was significant for several reasons, not least because Blackbaud's clientele includes a wide array of organizations that handle sensitive personal information. Among the affected entities were universities, healthcare providers, charities, and other non-profits, many of which rely on Blackbaud's systems to manage donor information, patient records, and other critical data. The attack compromised personal and financial data of millions of individuals, raising concerns about identity theft, financial fraud, and the broader implications for data privacy and security.

The initial stages of the attack involved the attackers gaining access to Blackbaud's systems through a compromised user account or vulnerability within their network. Once inside, the attackers deployed ransomware to encrypt files and demanded a ransom to prevent the public release of the stolen data. Blackbaud opted to pay the ransom, a decision that was widely criticized given the potential implications for encouraging future attacks and the uncertainty surrounding the attackers' commitment to honor their promises. The exact amount of the ransom payment was not disclosed, but it is believed to have been significant.

The data exfiltrated during the attack included a range of sensitive information such as names, addresses, phone numbers, email addresses, donation history, and in some cases, financial information like bank account details and Social Security numbers. The breach impacted a vast number of individuals globally, as many of Blackbaud's clients operate in multiple countries and handle data from international donors and supporters. The sheer volume and sensitivity of the compromised data underscored the critical importance of robust data security measures, particularly for organizations that manage large amounts of personal information.

One of the key aspects of the Blackbaud breach was the delayed disclosure of the incident. Blackbaud initially discovered the attack in May 2020 but did not publicly disclose it until July, leading to criticism from affected organizations and individuals regarding the lack of timely notification. This delay hindered the ability of impacted parties to take immediate steps to protect their data and mitigate potential risks, such as identity theft and fraud. The lack of prompt communication also raised questions about Blackbaud's transparency and commitment to data protection.

The breach's disclosure prompted widespread concern and scrutiny from regulatory bodies, affected organizations, and the public. Many organizations that relied on Blackbaud's services had to notify their stakeholders and comply with legal requirements regarding data breach notifications. This process involved significant time and resources, as affected entities worked to assess the impact of the breach, communicate with those affected, and implement measures to enhance their data security practices. The breach also highlighted the complex legal and regulatory landscape surrounding data breaches, with different jurisdictions imposing varying requirements for notification and remediation.

The regulatory response to the Blackbaud breach varied by region, with authorities in several countries launching investigations to assess the breach's impact and Blackbaud's compliance with data protection laws. In the United States, multiple states launched inquiries into the breach and its ramifications, while in Europe, regulators focused on potential violations of the General Data Protection Regulation (GDPR), which imposes stringent requirements for data protection and breach notification. The breach underscored the need for organizations to maintain a clear understanding of their legal obligations regarding data protection and to ensure that they are prepared to respond promptly and effectively to data breaches.

The Blackbaud ransomware attack also highlighted the broader implications of third-party risk in cybersecurity. Many organizations affected by the breach had entrusted Blackbaud with the management and security of their data, highlighting the critical importance of vetting and monitoring third-party vendors to ensure that they adhere to robust security practices. The breach underscored the need for organizations to conduct thorough risk assessments and to implement comprehensive vendor management programs to mitigate the risks associated with outsourcing data management and other critical functions to external providers.

In response to the breach, Blackbaud took several steps to enhance its security measures and to mitigate the risks of future attacks. The company announced plans to invest in additional security technologies, including advanced threat detection and response capabilities, and to strengthen its internal security protocols. Blackbaud also committed to improving its incident response procedures and to working more closely with its clients to ensure that they have the tools and resources needed to protect their data.

The breach also prompted affected organizations to reevaluate their data protection practices and to enhance their cybersecurity measures. Many organizations implemented additional security controls, such as multi-factor authentication, encryption, and regular security audits, to better protect their data and to reduce the risk of future breaches. The incident underscored the importance of maintaining a proactive approach to cybersecurity, including regular assessments of security risks and the implementation of best practices for data protection.

The Blackbaud breach also had significant implications for the broader cybersecurity landscape, highlighting the growing threat of ransomware and the need for a coordinated response to this evolving challenge. The incident underscored the importance of international cooperation in addressing cyber threats and the need for robust frameworks to facilitate information sharing and collaboration among governments, industry, and other stakeholders. The breach also highlighted the critical role of threat intelligence in identifying and mitigating cyber threats and the need for organizations to stay informed about emerging risks and vulnerabilities.

From a technological perspective, the Blackbaud breach underscored the importance of implementing advanced security measures to protect against sophisticated cyber threats. This includes the use of encryption to protect sensitive data both at rest and in transit, the deployment of advanced threat detection and response tools to identify and mitigate threats in real-time, and the adoption of zero-trust security models that assume all network traffic is potentially malicious and require continuous verification. The breach also highlighted the importance of regular security training and awareness programs for employees to ensure that they are aware of the risks and are equipped to respond effectively to potential threats.

The breach also underscored the importance of having a comprehensive incident response plan in place to effectively manage and mitigate the impact of data breaches. A well-prepared incident response plan can help organizations quickly identify and contain breaches, communicate effectively with stakeholders, and take appropriate steps to prevent further damage. The Blackbaud breach highlighted the need for organizations to regularly review and update their incident response plans to ensure that they are prepared to respond to evolving cyber threats and to protect their data and systems from potential breaches.

Chapter 33: Revil Ransomware

The REvil ransomware, also known as Sodinokibi, emerged as a significant threat in the cyber landscape in 2020, exemplifying the evolution of ransomware from relatively simplistic tools used by individual hackers into highly sophisticated and organized cybercrime operations. REvil became notorious for its aggressive tactics, widespread impact, and the significant financial losses it inflicted on organizations across the globe. The group's operations and the ensuing damage underscored the growing threat of ransomware and highlighted the challenges faced by cybersecurity professionals in combating these increasingly sophisticated and well-organized cybercriminal enterprises.

REvil is believed to have originated from a group of cybercriminals with roots in Russia. The group operated as a ransomware-as-a-service (RaaS) operation, a model where the developers of the ransomware provide the malware to affiliates who then carry out the attacks. The affiliates receive a share of the ransom payments, creating a highly lucrative and scalable business model. This approach allowed REvil to rapidly expand its operations and target a wide array of organizations across various sectors, including healthcare, finance, education, and critical infrastructure.

One of the distinguishing features of REvil was its use of double extortion tactics. Unlike traditional ransomware, which simply encrypts the victim's data and demands a ransom for the decryption key, REvil also exfiltrated sensitive data before encrypting it. The attackers then threatened to publish or sell the stolen data unless the ransom was paid, adding an additional layer of pressure on the victims. This tactic proved to be highly effective, as it leveraged the fear of sensitive data being exposed publicly or used for other malicious purposes to coerce victims into paying the ransom.

REvil's technical capabilities were formidable. The ransomware was designed to exploit vulnerabilities in various software systems to gain initial access to the victim's network. Once inside, it moved laterally to identify and exfiltrate valuable data before deploying the encryption payload. The malware used sophisticated encryption algorithms, making it nearly impossible to decrypt the files without the attacker's key. Additionally, REvil was equipped with features to detect and disable security software, complicating efforts to detect and remove the malware once it had infiltrated a network.

Throughout 2020, REvil was responsible for numerous high-profile attacks that had far-reaching consequences. One of the most notable incidents was the attack on the foreign currency exchange company Travelex in January. The attack led to a prolonged shutdown of Travelex's services, causing significant disruption and financial losses. The attackers demanded a ransom of $6 million, and the company was reportedly forced to pay a substantial sum to regain access to its systems and data. This incident highlighted the vulnerability of critical service providers to ransomware attacks and underscored the potential for significant economic damage.

Another significant attack attributed to REvil in 2020 targeted Grubman Shire Meiselas & Sacks, a prominent New York-based law firm specializing in media and entertainment. The attackers exfiltrated a vast amount of sensitive data, including contracts and personal information of high-profile clients such as Lady Gaga, Madonna, and Elton John. The attackers demanded a ransom of $42 million and threatened to release the stolen data if the firm did not comply. The breach attracted significant media attention and underscored the potential for ransomware to cause reputational damage and legal consequences, in addition to financial losses.

The REvil group also targeted healthcare organizations, which were particularly vulnerable during the COVID-19 pandemic. In May 2020, REvil attacked the German technology company Fresenius, one of the largest private hospital operators in Europe. The attack disrupted Fresenius's operations and highlighted the risk posed by ransomware to critical infrastructure and healthcare services during a time of heightened demand and vulnerability.

The scale and impact of REvil's attacks in 2020 were facilitated by the group's use of advanced and evolving tactics, techniques, and procedures (TTPs). REvil leveraged a variety of attack vectors to infiltrate networks, including phishing emails, exploit kits, and brute-force attacks on remote desktop protocol (RDP) services. The group also exploited vulnerabilities in widely used software, such as the Pulse Secure VPN, to gain access to targeted networks. Once inside, REvil used sophisticated tools to escalate privileges, evade detection, and move laterally within the network to maximize the impact of the attack.

One of the most concerning aspects of REvil's operations was its ability to innovate and adapt its tactics to stay ahead of defensive measures. The group regularly updated its malware to incorporate new features and to exploit emerging vulnerabilities. For instance, REvil's ransomware was designed to run on a variety of platforms, including Windows and Linux, allowing it to target a broad range of systems and environments. The group also employed techniques such as living off the land, which involves using legitimate administrative tools and commands to carry out malicious activities, making it more difficult for security teams to detect and respond to the attacks.

The impact of REvil's attacks extended beyond the immediate financial losses and operational disruptions experienced by the victims. The group's activities highlighted significant challenges for cybersecurity and raised important questions about how to effectively combat the growing threat of ransomware. The attacks underscored the need for organizations to adopt a multi-layered approach to cybersecurity, incorporating robust defenses, continuous monitoring, and rapid response capabilities to detect and mitigate threats before they can cause significant damage.

The REvil ransomware also highlighted the importance of a proactive approach to cybersecurity, including regular risk assessments, vulnerability management, and employee training to reduce the risk of successful attacks. Organizations were encouraged to implement best practices such as maintaining up-to-date backups, restricting access to sensitive data, and deploying advanced security technologies to detect and respond to threats in real-time. The incident underscored the critical role of threat intelligence in identifying and mitigating emerging threats and the need for organizations to stay informed about the latest developments in the threat landscape.

The legal and regulatory implications of the REvil attacks were also significant. The group's activities prompted calls for greater international cooperation and coordination to combat ransomware and other forms of cybercrime. Governments and law enforcement agencies around the world faced the challenge of tracking down and prosecuting the perpetrators, who often operated from jurisdictions with limited extradition agreements or legal frameworks for addressing cybercrime. The attacks highlighted the need for stronger legal frameworks and international agreements to facilitate the prosecution of cybercriminals and to hold them accountable for their actions.

The response to the REvil attacks also underscored the importance of public-private partnerships in addressing cybersecurity threats. Collaboration between government agencies, private sector organizations, and cybersecurity experts was critical in identifying and mitigating the threat posed by REvil. The sharing of threat intelligence, best practices, and resources was essential in enhancing the collective ability to defend against ransomware and other cyber threats.

The REvil ransomware attacks also had significant implications for the insurance industry. As the frequency and severity of ransomware attacks increased, many organizations turned to cyber insurance to mitigate the financial impact of potential breaches. However, the growing cost of ransomware claims and the evolving threat landscape prompted insurers to reassess their coverage and pricing models. The REvil attacks highlighted the need for insurers to incorporate more stringent risk assessments and to incentivize organizations to adopt robust cybersecurity measures to reduce the likelihood of successful attacks.

In the aftermath of the REvil attacks, there was a growing recognition of the need for a comprehensive approach to ransomware prevention and response. This included not only technical measures but also policy and legal initiatives to address the underlying factors that contribute to the prevalence of ransomware. Governments and industry stakeholders were encouraged to work together to develop strategies for disrupting the financial incentives that drive ransomware attacks, such as cracking down on the use of cryptocurrencies for ransom payments and enhancing efforts to trace and recover stolen funds.

The REvil ransomware attacks also prompted discussions about the ethical and policy implications of paying ransoms. While some organizations felt compelled to pay ransoms to regain access to their data and minimize operational disruptions, there were concerns that such payments incentivized further attacks and contributed to the profitability of ransomware operations. The debate highlighted the need for clearer guidelines and policies regarding ransom payments and the importance of developing alternative strategies for dealing with ransomware incidents.

Chapter 34: Colonial Pipeline Ransomware Attack

The Colonial Pipeline ransomware attack of May 2021 marked one of the most significant cybersecurity incidents in recent history, drawing widespread attention to the vulnerabilities in critical infrastructure and highlighting the severe consequences that can arise from cyberattacks on essential services. This attack, which disrupted the largest fuel pipeline system in the United States, underscored the profound impact of ransomware on public safety, the economy, and national security. The incident spurred a flurry of responses from government and industry leaders, prompting a renewed focus on cybersecurity for critical infrastructure. The Colonial Pipeline attack serves as a case study in the complexities of modern cyber threats and the urgent need for robust cybersecurity measures to protect essential services from future attacks.

Colonial Pipeline, a major player in the U.S. energy sector, operates a sprawling network that transports gasoline, diesel, and jet fuel from refineries on the Gulf Coast to various markets across the southern and eastern United States. The pipeline system, spanning more than 5,500 miles, supplies nearly half of the fuel consumed on the East Coast, making it a critical component of the nation's energy infrastructure. Given its importance, any disruption to the pipeline's operations has significant implications for fuel supply, prices, and economic stability.

The attack began on May 7, 2021, when Colonial Pipeline's IT systems were infiltrated by a group of cybercriminals known as DarkSide. This group, which operates as a ransomware-as-a-service (RaaS) entity, had developed a sophisticated ransomware strain capable of encrypting files and demanding ransom payments in exchange for decryption keys. DarkSide's model involved leasing their ransomware to affiliates, who would then carry out attacks and share the profits with the developers, creating a scalable and lucrative business model for cybercrime.

The attackers gained access to Colonial Pipeline's systems through a compromised password linked to an old virtual private network (VPN) account that did not use multi-factor authentication (MFA). This access allowed the attackers to navigate the network, identify critical data, and deploy the ransomware, which began encrypting files and effectively crippling the company's IT operations. The encryption rendered critical data inaccessible and disrupted the flow of fuel through the pipeline, forcing Colonial Pipeline to shut down its entire system to prevent the malware from spreading further.

The decision to shut down the pipeline was made to contain the threat and protect operational systems from being compromised, but it also had immediate and widespread repercussions. The shutdown led to significant disruptions in fuel supply, causing panic buying and fuel shortages across the East Coast. Gasoline prices surged to their highest levels in years, and long lines formed at gas stations as consumers rushed to fill their tanks. The situation highlighted the interconnectedness of critical infrastructure and the cascading effects that can result from disruptions in essential services.

In response to the attack, Colonial Pipeline engaged cybersecurity experts and law enforcement agencies, including the FBI, to assist in investigating the breach and restoring operations. The company also took the controversial step of paying a ransom of approximately $4.4 million in Bitcoin to the attackers in exchange for a decryption key. The decision to pay the ransom was criticized by many experts and policymakers, as it potentially incentivized further attacks and contributed to the profitability of ransomware operations. Despite the payment, the decryption process was slow and challenging, and it took several days for Colonial Pipeline to fully restore its systems and resume normal operations.

The Colonial Pipeline attack underscored several critical issues and vulnerabilities in the realm of cybersecurity for critical infrastructure. One of the primary lessons was the importance of securing access points and using strong authentication measures. The attack exploited a weak password and the lack of MFA on a VPN account, highlighting the need for robust access controls and continuous monitoring of network activity to detect and respond to threats promptly.

The incident also highlighted the risks associated with legacy systems and outdated software. Many critical infrastructure organizations, including Colonial Pipeline, rely on legacy systems that may lack the security features and updates necessary to defend against modern cyber threats. The attack underscored the importance of regularly updating and patching systems to address known vulnerabilities and to ensure that security measures keep pace with evolving threats.

Another key takeaway from the Colonial Pipeline attack was the critical need for incident response planning and preparedness. The disruption caused by the attack demonstrated the importance of having a comprehensive incident response plan in place to quickly contain and mitigate the impact of cyber incidents. This includes conducting regular drills and exercises to test response capabilities and ensure that all stakeholders are prepared to act swiftly and effectively in the event of a cyberattack.

The attack also raised important questions about the role of government and industry in protecting critical infrastructure from cyber threats. In the wake of the incident, there were calls for greater collaboration and information sharing between the public and private sectors to enhance the resilience of critical infrastructure. The U.S. government took several steps to address these concerns, including issuing an executive order to improve the nation's cybersecurity and to mandate stronger security measures for critical infrastructure operators.

One of the significant regulatory responses to the attack was the introduction of new cybersecurity directives by the Transportation Security Administration (TSA) for pipeline operators. These directives required pipeline companies to report cybersecurity incidents to the Cybersecurity and Infrastructure Security Agency (CISA) within specified timeframes, conduct vulnerability assessments, and implement cybersecurity measures to protect against ransomware and other threats. The directives aimed to enhance the security of the nation's energy infrastructure and to ensure that operators are prepared to respond to and recover from cyber incidents.

The Colonial Pipeline attack also underscored the importance of supply chain security. The disruption of fuel supplies had a cascading effect on various sectors, including transportation, retail, and healthcare, highlighting the interdependencies within the supply chain and the potential for cyberattacks to cause widespread disruption. The incident emphasized the need for a holistic approach to cybersecurity that considers the entire supply chain and the potential impacts of disruptions on critical services and infrastructure.

From a technological perspective, the attack highlighted the need for advanced security measures to detect and mitigate threats. This includes the use of intrusion detection systems, endpoint detection and response (EDR) tools, and threat intelligence to identify and respond to threats in real time. The incident also underscored the importance of network segmentation to limit the spread of malware and to protect critical systems from being compromised.

The Colonial Pipeline attack had significant economic implications, not only in terms of the direct costs associated with the ransom payment and the disruption of operations but also in the broader impact on fuel prices and consumer confidence. The incident highlighted the potential for cyberattacks to cause substantial economic damage and underscored the importance of investing in cybersecurity to protect against such threats. The economic impact of the attack also raised awareness of the need for businesses and organizations to consider cybersecurity as a critical component of risk management and to allocate resources accordingly to protect their operations and assets.

The attack also had important legal and policy implications. The decision to pay the ransom raised questions about the legality and ethics of making ransom payments and the potential for such payments to fund criminal activities. The incident highlighted the need for clearer guidelines and policies regarding ransomware payments and the importance of developing alternative strategies for dealing with ransomware incidents. The attack also prompted discussions about the need for stronger legal frameworks and international cooperation to combat ransomware and other forms of cybercrime.

Chapter 35: Kaseya VSA Ransomware Attack

The Kaseya VSA ransomware attack in July 2021 stands as a stark reminder of the vulnerabilities inherent in supply chain dependencies and the catastrophic potential of sophisticated cyber assaults. Orchestrated by the notorious REvil ransomware group, also known as Sodinokibi, the attack leveraged a zero-day vulnerability in Kaseya's VSA software, a widely used remote monitoring and management (RMM) tool, to unleash a widespread ransomware campaign. This incident highlighted the intricate complexities of cybersecurity in modern interconnected environments and underscored the critical importance of robust security practices, rapid response mechanisms, and international cooperation in combating cyber threats.

Kaseya, a leading provider of IT management solutions, offers the VSA software to managed service providers (MSPs) and IT departments. This software is designed to streamline the management of networks and systems, enabling remote monitoring, patch management, and automation of routine IT tasks. MSPs, which use Kaseya VSA to manage IT services for multiple clients, became unwitting vectors for the attack, which cascaded down to numerous end-user organizations. The Kaseya VSA attack thus exemplifies the risks associated with supply chain attacks, where a compromise in a single supplier or service provider can have far-reaching implications across multiple organizations.

The REvil group, a cybercriminal gang with a history of high-profile ransomware attacks, exploited a previously unknown (zero-day) vulnerability in the Kaseya VSA software. This vulnerability allowed the attackers to gain administrative access to the VSA servers and inject malicious scripts into the VSA software update mechanism. When the compromised updates were deployed, they installed the

REvil ransomware on the networks of the MSPs and their clients, encrypting data and disrupting operations.

The attack began on July 2, 2021, and quickly spread, affecting approximately 60 MSPs and up to 1,500 of their clients worldwide. The timing of the attack, on the eve of a major U.S. holiday weekend, was strategically chosen to maximize impact and minimize the likelihood of a rapid response. Many affected organizations, which ranged from small businesses to larger enterprises across various sectors, were forced to shut down operations and initiate extensive recovery efforts. The attackers demanded a ransom of $70 million in Bitcoin in exchange for a universal decryption key that could unlock all affected systems. This unprecedented ransom demand underscored the scale and ambition of the attack.

The immediate impact of the Kaseya VSA attack was profound, causing significant operational disruptions for affected organizations. Businesses across various sectors, including healthcare, retail, and public services, experienced downtime and data loss. For instance, Coop, a major supermarket chain in Sweden, was forced to close over 800 stores as the attack disrupted its cash register systems. The incident highlighted the vulnerability of critical infrastructure and essential services to cyber threats and underscored the need for robust cybersecurity measures to protect against such disruptions.

The response to the Kaseya VSA attack involved a coordinated effort from multiple stakeholders, including Kaseya, cybersecurity firms, and government agencies. Kaseya promptly took its cloud-based VSA service offline and urged on-premises users to shut down their VSA servers to prevent further spread of the ransomware. The company worked closely with the FBI, CISA (Cybersecurity and Infrastructure Security Agency), and other law enforcement agencies to investigate the breach and to identify and mitigate the vulnerabilities exploited by the attackers. Cybersecurity firms like FireEye, Sophos, and ESET provided critical support in analyzing the malware, developing detection and remediation tools, and assisting affected organizations in their recovery efforts.

Kaseya's handling of the attack drew both praise and criticism. The company was lauded for its transparency and swift action in shutting down its services to contain the attack and for its efforts in providing regular updates and support to affected customers. However, some criticized Kaseya for not addressing the vulnerability sooner, despite warnings from cybersecurity researchers who had identified potential weaknesses in the VSA software. This aspect of the incident highlighted the importance of proactive vulnerability management and the need for organizations to respond promptly to security advisories and to implement patches and updates to mitigate risks.

The Kaseya VSA attack also underscored the critical importance of supply chain security. The attackers leveraged Kaseya's trusted relationship with its customers to distribute the ransomware widely and rapidly. This type of attack, where a compromise in a single supplier can have cascading effects across multiple organizations, highlights the vulnerabilities in modern supply chains and the need for robust security measures to protect against such threats. Organizations were encouraged to conduct thorough risk assessments of their supply chains, to implement stringent security controls, and to engage in continuous monitoring and assessment of their suppliers' security practices.

The incident prompted a broader discussion about the role of cybersecurity in critical infrastructure and the need for greater investment in security measures to protect essential services. Governments and regulatory bodies emphasized the need for enhanced cybersecurity standards and requirements for critical infrastructure operators, including mandatory incident reporting, regular vulnerability assessments, and the adoption of best practices for cybersecurity. The attack also highlighted the need for public-private partnerships to enhance the resilience of critical infrastructure and to facilitate the sharing of threat intelligence and best practices.

The Kaseya VSA attack also had significant implications for the cybersecurity landscape, highlighting the evolving tactics and techniques used by ransomware groups. The use of zero-day vulnerabilities and the exploitation of trusted relationships between service providers and their customers exemplify the increasing sophistication of cyber threats. The attack underscored the need for organizations to adopt a multi-layered approach to cybersecurity, including the use of advanced threat detection and response tools, continuous monitoring of network activity, and regular training and awareness programs for employees to identify and respond to threats.

From a technological perspective, the attack highlighted the importance of adopting advanced security measures to detect and mitigate threats. Organizations were encouraged to implement endpoint detection and response (EDR) tools, intrusion detection systems, and other advanced security technologies to identify and respond to threats in real time. The incident also underscored the importance of network segmentation to limit the spread of malware and to protect critical systems from being compromised. Additionally, organizations were advised to implement robust backup and disaster recovery solutions to ensure that data could be quickly restored in the event of an attack.

The legal and policy implications of the Kaseya VSA attack were also significant. The incident highlighted the need for clearer guidelines and policies regarding ransomware payments and the potential for such payments to incentivize further attacks. Governments and policymakers were encouraged to develop strategies for disrupting the financial incentives that drive ransomware attacks, including measures to regulate and trace cryptocurrency transactions used for ransom payments. The attack also underscored the importance of international cooperation in combating cybercrime and the need for stronger legal frameworks to hold cybercriminals accountable for their actions.

The attack also had significant implications for the insurance industry, as organizations increasingly looked to cyber insurance to mitigate the financial impact of ransomware attacks. The growing frequency and severity of ransomware attacks prompted insurers to reassess their coverage and pricing models, and to encourage policyholders to adopt stronger cybersecurity measures to reduce the likelihood of successful attacks. The Kaseya VSA attack highlighted the importance of incorporating comprehensive risk assessments and cybersecurity best practices into insurance underwriting processes to enhance the overall security posture of insured organizations.

Chapter 36: T-Mobile Data Breach

The T-Mobile data breach of 2021 stands as one of the most significant and wide-reaching cyber incidents in recent memory, affecting millions of customers and highlighting critical vulnerabilities in corporate cybersecurity practices. The breach, which was publicly disclosed in August 2021, involved the theft of sensitive personal information from approximately 76.6 million individuals, including current, former, and prospective T-Mobile customers. This massive data breach underscored the importance of robust data protection measures and the growing threat of cyberattacks targeting large corporations. It also prompted significant scrutiny and criticism of T-Mobile's cybersecurity practices and raised important questions about data privacy and security in the digital age.

T-Mobile, one of the largest wireless carriers in the United States, serves tens of millions of customers and manages vast amounts of personal data. This data includes not only customer contact information but also sensitive details such as Social Security numbers, driver's license information, and financial data. The sheer volume and sensitivity of the data make telecommunications companies like T-Mobile prime targets for cybercriminals seeking to exploit personal information for financial gain or other malicious purposes.

The breach was first reported by a security researcher who discovered that a hacker was selling a large cache of T-Mobile's customer data on an underground forum. The hacker claimed to have obtained the data by exploiting vulnerabilities in T-Mobile's systems, specifically gaining unauthorized access to a poorly secured server. The hacker reportedly offered to sell the data for several Bitcoin, highlighting the value and market for stolen personal information in the cybercriminal underground.

Upon learning of the breach, T-Mobile launched an investigation and confirmed that unauthorized access to its systems had occurred.

The company disclosed that personal information from approximately 40 million current and former customers, as well as approximately 36.6 million prospective customers who had applied for credit, had been compromised. The data exposed in the breach included names, birthdates, Social Security numbers, driver's license information, phone numbers, and other sensitive details. Additionally, the breach affected over 850,000 active T-Mobile prepaid customers, whose names, phone numbers, and account PINs were also exposed.

The scale and severity of the T-Mobile data breach had significant implications for affected individuals. The exposure of sensitive personal information, such as Social Security numbers and driver's license details, increased the risk of identity theft and financial fraud. Criminals could potentially use this information to open fraudulent accounts, apply for loans or credit, or engage in other forms of identity theft. The breach also highlighted the potential for further exploitation, as personal information could be used for targeted phishing attacks, social engineering, and other malicious activities.

In response to the breach, T-Mobile offered affected customers two years of free credit monitoring and identity protection services. The company also provided guidance on steps individuals could take to protect themselves from identity theft, such as placing fraud alerts on their credit files, monitoring their accounts for suspicious activity, and changing their account PINs and passwords. However, many affected individuals expressed frustration and concern, feeling that these measures were insufficient to fully address the long-term risks posed by the exposure of their personal information.

The T-Mobile data breach also prompted significant criticism of the company's cybersecurity practices and raised questions about how the breach could have occurred. Critics pointed to the company's history of data breaches, noting that this was not the first time T-Mobile had experienced a significant security incident. In fact, T-Mobile had suffered several previous breaches, including incidents in

2018, 2019, and 2020, which had also exposed customer data. These repeated breaches highlighted potential weaknesses in the company's security posture and raised concerns about the effectiveness of its data protection measures.

The breach underscored the importance of strong cybersecurity practices and the need for companies to continuously assess and improve their security measures to protect against evolving threats. Key areas of focus include the implementation of robust access controls, regular vulnerability assessments, and the use of advanced security technologies to detect and respond to threats in real time. The incident also highlighted the importance of encryption and other data protection measures to safeguard sensitive information, both in transit and at rest.

From a technological perspective, the T-Mobile data breach highlighted the importance of securing access to sensitive systems and data. The breach reportedly involved the exploitation of a vulnerability in an unprotected server, underscoring the need for comprehensive security measures to protect against unauthorized access. This includes the use of strong authentication mechanisms, such as multi-factor authentication (MFA), to prevent unauthorized access to systems and data. Additionally, companies are encouraged to adopt a zero-trust security model, which assumes that threats can originate from both external and internal sources, and therefore requires continuous verification of all users and devices accessing the network.

The breach also highlighted the need for effective incident response and recovery capabilities. The ability to quickly detect and respond to security incidents is critical to minimizing the impact of a breach and preventing further data loss. Organizations are encouraged to develop and regularly test their incident response plans, conduct regular security drills and exercises, and ensure that all stakeholders are prepared to respond to security incidents in a coordinated and effective manner.

The T-Mobile data breach had significant legal and regulatory implications as well. The incident prompted several lawsuits from affected individuals and groups, alleging that T-Mobile had failed to adequately protect their personal information and seeking compensation for the harm caused by the breach. The lawsuits highlighted the potential for significant legal and financial consequences for companies that fail to protect customer data and underscored the importance of compliance with data protection regulations and standards.

In response to the breach, regulatory bodies and lawmakers called for stronger data protection measures and greater accountability for companies that handle sensitive personal information. The incident highlighted the need for comprehensive data protection laws and regulations to ensure that companies take appropriate measures to safeguard customer data and to hold them accountable for breaches. This includes requirements for data encryption, regular security assessments, and timely notification of affected individuals in the event of a breach.

The breach also prompted discussions about the role of cybersecurity in corporate governance and the importance of executive accountability for data protection. Organizations were encouraged to integrate cybersecurity into their overall risk management and governance frameworks, to ensure that data protection is a priority at all levels of the organization. This includes the appointment of dedicated cybersecurity professionals, such as Chief Information Security Officers (CISOs), and the implementation of comprehensive security policies and procedures to protect against threats.

The T-Mobile data breach also had significant implications for the insurance industry. As companies increasingly face the threat of cyberattacks, the demand for cyber insurance has grown. The breach highlighted the importance of comprehensive cyber insurance coverage to mitigate the financial impact of data breaches and other cyber incidents. Insurers were encouraged to assess the cybersecurity practices of their clients and to provide guidance on best practices for data protection and incident response.

The breach also underscored the importance of transparency and communication in the aftermath of a data breach. T-Mobile's response to the breach, including its public disclosures and communication with affected customers, was critical to managing the incident and mitigating the impact on its reputation. Organizations are encouraged to develop and implement communication plans as part of their incident response strategies, to ensure that they can effectively communicate with stakeholders and the public in the event of a breach.

Chapter 37: Facebook Data Leak

The Facebook data leak of 2021, also known as the Facebook "Data Scraping Incident," represents one of the most significant breaches of personal information in recent history, affecting over 530 million users worldwide. This incident, which was publicly revealed in April 2021, exposed a massive trove of user data that included personal details such as phone numbers, email addresses, and other profile information. The leak, although initially stemming from data scraping activities in 2019, underscored the critical challenges associated with data privacy and the security of user information on social media platforms. It also brought to light the vulnerabilities in data protection practices and raised urgent questions about the responsibilities of tech giants like Facebook in safeguarding user data.

The data leak was first brought to public attention by Alon Gal, co-founder of the cybersecurity firm Hudson Rock, who discovered a large dataset containing personal information of Facebook users being offered for free on a hacking forum. The data, which had been compiled by malicious actors through a process known as data scraping, included information from 533 million Facebook users from 106 countries. This vast dataset comprised phone numbers, Facebook IDs, full names, locations, birthdates, bios, and, in some cases, email addresses. The sheer scale and scope of the exposed information highlighted the extensive reach of the breach and the potential for significant misuse of the data by cybercriminals and malicious actors.

Data scraping involves the automated extraction of data from websites and online platforms, often using bots or automated scripts to gather information that is publicly accessible or poorly protected. In this case, the data was scraped from Facebook profiles through a vulnerability in the platform's contact importer feature. This feature, which was intended to help users find and connect with friends by importing their contact lists, allowed malicious actors to exploit a flaw and retrieve vast amounts of user data without authorization. Although the vulnerability was patched by Facebook in August 2019, the data that had already been collected continued to circulate and eventually became publicly accessible in 2021.

The exposed data included a variety of personal information that could be used for various malicious purposes. For instance, the availability of phone numbers opened the door to phishing attacks, where attackers could impersonate trusted entities and deceive users into providing sensitive information or clicking on malicious links. The data could also be used for targeted spam campaigns, identity theft, and other forms of cybercrime. Additionally, the availability of detailed personal information, such as birthdates and locations, increased the risk of social engineering attacks, where attackers manipulate individuals into divulging confidential information or performing actions that compromise security.

The revelation of the data leak prompted widespread concern and criticism of Facebook's data protection practices. Critics argued that Facebook had failed to adequately protect user data and that the company should have taken more proactive measures to prevent such large-scale scraping activities. The incident also highlighted the challenges of securing personal information on social media platforms, where user data is often publicly accessible or shared with a wide audience. The ease with which the data was scraped and the subsequent public availability of the information underscored the need for stronger security measures and better user privacy controls.

In response to the data leak, Facebook issued a statement acknowledging the incident and emphasizing that the data had been scraped due to a vulnerability that had been fixed in 2019. The company stressed that the exposed data was not the result of a hack or a breach of its security systems, but rather the outcome of automated scraping by malicious actors. Facebook also pointed out that the exposed data was not sensitive, such as passwords or financial information, but rather information that users had chosen to share on their profiles. However, this explanation did little to assuage public concerns, as the vast amount of personal information exposed still posed significant risks to affected users.

Facebook's response to the incident also included efforts to improve its data protection practices and to prevent similar incidents in the future. The company announced that it would enhance its security measures, including the implementation of stricter access controls and more robust monitoring of scraping activities. Facebook also committed to improving its transparency and communication with users about data privacy issues, including providing clearer information about how user data is collected, used, and protected on the platform.

The Facebook data leak also raised important questions about the legal and regulatory frameworks governing data privacy and security. In many jurisdictions, companies that handle personal information are required to comply with data protection laws and regulations, such as the General Data Protection Regulation (GDPR) in the European Union and the California Consumer Privacy Act (CCPA) in the United States. These regulations mandate that companies implement appropriate security measures to protect personal data and that they notify affected individuals in the event of a data breach. The Facebook data leak highlighted potential gaps in these regulatory frameworks, particularly in terms of addressing the risks associated with data scraping and ensuring that companies take proactive measures to prevent unauthorized access to user data.

The incident also underscored the importance of user awareness and education about data privacy and security. Many users are not fully aware of the risks associated with sharing personal information online or the potential for their data to be scraped and misused by malicious actors. The Facebook data leak highlighted the need for greater user education about how to protect their personal information and the importance of using privacy settings to control who can access their data. Users were encouraged to review their privacy settings on social media platforms, to limit the amount of personal information they share publicly, and to be cautious about accepting friend requests or sharing their contact information with unknown individuals.

The data leak also had significant implications for the cybersecurity community and the broader tech industry. It highlighted the need for companies to invest in advanced security technologies and practices to protect user data from scraping and other forms of unauthorized access. This includes the use of artificial intelligence and machine learning to detect and prevent scraping activities, as well as the implementation of stronger encryption and access controls to safeguard sensitive information. The incident also underscored the importance of collaboration and information sharing among companies, cybersecurity firms, and government agencies to address emerging threats and to enhance the overall security of online platforms.

From a technological perspective, the Facebook data leak highlighted the challenges of securing large-scale online platforms and the need for continuous improvement in security practices. Social media platforms like Facebook handle vast amounts of user data and are constantly evolving to accommodate new features and functionality. This dynamic environment creates opportunities for malicious actors to exploit vulnerabilities and access user data. Companies are encouraged to adopt a proactive approach to security, including regular vulnerability assessments, continuous monitoring of network activity, and the implementation of advanced threat detection and response capabilities.

The incident also highlighted the importance of ethical considerations in data collection and use. The widespread availability of personal information through data scraping raises questions about the ethical implications of collecting and using data without user consent. Companies are encouraged to adopt ethical data practices that prioritize user privacy and to ensure that their data collection and use practices are transparent and aligned with user expectations. This includes obtaining informed consent from users for data collection, providing clear information about how data is used and shared, and implementing measures to protect user data from unauthorized access.

The Facebook data leak also prompted discussions about the role of government and policymakers in protecting data privacy and security. There were calls for stronger regulatory oversight and enforcement to ensure that companies take appropriate measures to protect user data and to hold them accountable for data breaches. Policymakers were encouraged to consider new regulations and guidelines to address the risks associated with data scraping and to ensure that companies implement robust security measures to protect personal information. The incident also highlighted the need for international cooperation to address the global nature of cyber threats and to promote best practices for data protection and security.

Chapter 38: Robinhood Data Breach

The Robinhood data breach of 2021 is a profound example of the intricate challenges faced by modern financial technology companies in safeguarding user data against increasingly sophisticated cyber threats. On November 3, 2021, Robinhood Markets, Inc., a popular online brokerage firm known for democratizing investment access through commission-free trading, announced a significant security incident that compromised the personal information of millions of its users. The breach not only exposed sensitive customer data but also underscored the critical importance of robust cybersecurity practices, transparency, and the implications of data privacy in the rapidly evolving fintech landscape.

Robinhood, founded in 2013, has become a prominent name in the fintech industry, attracting millions of retail investors with its user-friendly mobile app and zero-commission trading model. By 2021, the platform boasted over 22.5 million users, handling substantial amounts of sensitive personal and financial data. This rapid growth, while demonstrating the platform's success, also made it an attractive target for cybercriminals seeking to exploit vulnerabilities in its security infrastructure.

The breach occurred through a sophisticated social engineering attack that targeted a Robinhood customer support representative. The attackers were able to manipulate the employee into providing access to specific internal systems. Social engineering attacks often rely on psychological manipulation, tricking individuals into divulging confidential information or performing actions that compromise security. In this case, the attackers utilized social engineering techniques to bypass security protocols, gaining unauthorized access to Robinhood's internal systems and ultimately exfiltrating customer data.

Once inside the system, the attackers were able to access a significant amount of user data. According to Robinhood's disclosure, the breach exposed the personal information of approximately 7 million users. For 5 million of these users, email addresses were exposed, and for an additional 2 million users, their full names were compromised. More critically, for approximately 310 users, additional personal information such as date of birth and zip codes was exposed. Moreover, for about 10 users, even more extensive account details were accessed, raising significant concerns about potential identity theft and financial fraud.

The breach's immediate impact was multifaceted, affecting not only the individuals whose data was exposed but also raising broader concerns about the security practices of financial technology platforms. The exposed data, particularly email addresses and full names, increased the risk of targeted phishing attacks, where cybercriminals could use the information to craft convincing fraudulent emails to deceive users into providing further sensitive information or clicking on malicious links. The exposure of more detailed personal information for some users further heightened the risk of identity theft and fraud, potentially allowing criminals to open new accounts or make unauthorized transactions in the victims' names.

In response to the breach, Robinhood took several immediate actions to mitigate the impact and enhance its security posture. The company promptly notified law enforcement and engaged Mandiant, a leading cybersecurity firm, to assist in investigating the breach and to provide expertise in securing its systems against further threats. Robinhood also communicated with affected users, providing information about the nature of the breach and the specific data that had been exposed. The company offered affected users identity protection services, including credit monitoring and identity theft protection, to help them safeguard their personal information against potential misuse.

The breach also prompted Robinhood to reassess its internal security measures and to implement additional safeguards to protect user data. The company emphasized its commitment to security and privacy, highlighting efforts to enhance its cybersecurity infrastructure and to prevent future incidents. Key measures included strengthening access controls, improving security training for employees to better recognize and respond to social engineering attacks, and implementing more advanced threat detection and response capabilities to identify and mitigate potential threats in real time.

The Robinhood data breach also highlighted the broader challenges associated with data privacy and security in the fintech industry. As fintech companies continue to grow and handle increasing amounts of sensitive personal and financial data, they face significant pressure to maintain robust security measures to protect against evolving cyber threats. The incident underscored the importance of adopting a proactive approach to cybersecurity, including regular vulnerability assessments, continuous monitoring, and the implementation of comprehensive security policies and procedures.

From a regulatory perspective, the breach raised important questions about the adequacy of existing data protection frameworks and the need for stricter regulatory oversight of fintech companies. In many jurisdictions, financial institutions and fintech companies are subject to stringent data protection regulations, such as the General Data Protection Regulation (GDPR) in the European Union and the California Consumer Privacy Act (CCPA) in the United States. These regulations require companies to implement appropriate security measures to protect personal data and to notify affected individuals in the event of a data breach. The Robinhood breach highlighted potential gaps in these regulatory frameworks, particularly concerning the ability of fintech companies to effectively manage and secure large volumes of user data.

The breach also had significant implications for user trust and the reputation of Robinhood as a leading fintech platform. Trust is a critical component of the relationship between financial institutions and their customers, and any breach of that trust can have long-lasting repercussions. The incident prompted concerns among users about the security of their personal and financial information and raised questions about Robinhood's ability to protect its users' data. The company's response to the breach, including its transparency and efforts to improve its security practices, was crucial in managing the impact on its reputation and in rebuilding user trust.

From a technological standpoint, the Robinhood data breach underscored the importance of robust security practices to protect against sophisticated cyber threats. Key areas of focus for fintech companies include the implementation of strong authentication mechanisms, such as multi-factor authentication (MFA), to prevent unauthorized access to systems and data. Companies are also encouraged to adopt a zero-trust security model, which assumes that threats can originate from both internal and external sources, and therefore requires continuous verification of all users and devices accessing the network. Additionally, the use of advanced encryption techniques to protect sensitive data, both in transit and at rest, is critical to ensuring that data remains secure even if it is accessed by unauthorized individuals.

The breach also highlighted the importance of employee training and awareness in preventing social engineering attacks. Social engineering exploits human psychology to bypass technical security measures, and effective training can help employees recognize and respond to such threats. Fintech companies are encouraged to implement regular security training programs for employees, including simulated phishing exercises and other practical scenarios, to ensure that employees are prepared to identify and mitigate potential threats.

The Robinhood data breach also had significant implications for the insurance industry. As cyber threats continue to evolve, the demand for cyber insurance has grown, with companies seeking to mitigate the financial impact of data breaches and other cyber incidents. The breach highlighted the importance of comprehensive cyber insurance coverage for fintech companies, including coverage for the costs associated with breach response, identity protection services, and legal liabilities. Insurers were encouraged to assess the cybersecurity practices of their clients and to provide guidance on best practices for data protection and incident response.

The legal implications of the breach were also significant, with potential for regulatory investigations and lawsuits from affected individuals and groups. The breach highlighted the need for clear guidelines and policies regarding data protection and the responsibilities of companies in safeguarding user data. Legal experts emphasized the importance of compliance with data protection regulations and the potential for significant legal and financial consequences for companies that fail to protect customer data.

The Robinhood data breach also prompted discussions about the role of government and policymakers in protecting data privacy and security. There were calls for stronger regulatory oversight and enforcement to ensure that fintech companies take appropriate measures to protect user data and to hold them accountable for data breaches. Policymakers were encouraged to consider new regulations and guidelines to address the risks associated with data breaches and to ensure that companies implement robust security measures to protect personal information.

Chapter 39: Accellion FTA Breach

The Accellion FTA breach of 2021 stands as a striking example of the vulnerabilities inherent in legacy software systems and the profound implications such breaches can have on data security, privacy, and organizational integrity. The incident, which unfolded over the course of several months, involved the compromise of a file transfer application (FTA) developed by Accellion, a company that provides secure file sharing and collaboration solutions. This breach not only exposed sensitive information from a wide range of organizations but also underscored the complexities and challenges associated with maintaining and securing aging technological infrastructure.

Accellion, founded in 1999, specializes in secure file transfer and content collaboration solutions, with its FTA being a cornerstone product for many years. The FTA, designed to facilitate the secure exchange of large files, was widely adopted across various industries, including healthcare, government, financial services, and higher education. Despite its extensive use, the FTA had been classified as a legacy product by Accellion and was set to be discontinued in favor of the company's more modern and robust solution, Kiteworks. The decision to phase out the FTA was partly due to the inherent limitations and security challenges associated with maintaining older software.

The breach began in December 2020, when threat actors exploited several zero-day vulnerabilities in the Accellion FTA. Zero-day vulnerabilities are security flaws that are unknown to the software vendor and thus have no existing patch or fix at the time of their discovery. In this case, the attackers were able to identify and exploit multiple zero-day vulnerabilities in the FTA, allowing them to gain unauthorized access to the system and exfiltrate sensitive data. The initial attack was sophisticated and well-coordinated, targeting specific organizations that were known to use the FTA for their file transfer needs.

The attackers were part of a sophisticated criminal group, later linked to the notorious FIN11 and Clop ransomware gangs, known for their expertise in exploiting vulnerabilities to gain access to sensitive information and demanding ransom payments. Once inside the FTA, the attackers were able to access and download a wide range of sensitive files, including personal information, financial data, and confidential documents. The attackers then proceeded to deploy web shells, malicious scripts that allowed them to maintain persistent access to the compromised systems, facilitating further data exfiltration and manipulation.

The scope of the breach was extensive, affecting over 100 organizations worldwide, including prominent institutions such as the University of Colorado, the Reserve Bank of New Zealand, the Office of the Washington State Auditor, and major healthcare providers like Kroger and Centene. The exposed data varied widely in nature and sensitivity, with some organizations reporting the loss of highly confidential information, including Social Security numbers, driver's license numbers, medical records, and financial statements. The breach highlighted the broad impact that a single vulnerability in a widely used software product could have across multiple sectors and regions.

One of the critical aspects of the Accellion FTA breach was the attackers' use of extortion tactics to further exploit the compromised data. In many cases, the threat actors contacted the affected organizations, threatening to publicly release the stolen data unless a ransom was paid. This tactic, known as double extortion, is commonly used by sophisticated cybercriminal groups to maximize their financial gain from data breaches. The threat of public exposure not only pressured organizations to pay the ransom but also raised significant concerns about the potential reputational damage and legal liabilities associated with the breach.

The response to the breach involved a multifaceted effort to contain the damage, identify the vulnerabilities, and enhance security measures to prevent further exploitation. Accellion worked closely with external cybersecurity experts and law enforcement agencies to investigate the incident and to develop and deploy patches to address the vulnerabilities. The company also communicated with its affected customers, providing guidance on securing their systems and mitigating the impact of the breach. Additionally, Accellion accelerated its plans to transition customers from the FTA to the more secure Kiteworks platform, emphasizing the importance of upgrading to newer, more secure software solutions.

The breach also prompted affected organizations to conduct thorough assessments of their security practices and to implement additional safeguards to protect sensitive data. Many organizations undertook comprehensive security audits to identify potential vulnerabilities in their systems and to strengthen their defenses against similar attacks. This included enhancing access controls, implementing advanced threat detection and response capabilities, and increasing employee awareness and training to recognize and respond to potential security threats.

From a regulatory perspective, the Accellion FTA breach highlighted the critical importance of compliance with data protection laws and the need for robust security measures to protect sensitive information. Many of the affected organizations were subject to stringent data protection regulations, such as the General Data Protection Regulation (GDPR) in the European Union and the Health Insurance Portability and Accountability Act (HIPAA) in the United States. These regulations require organizations to implement appropriate security measures to protect personal data and to report data breaches to the relevant authorities and affected individuals. The breach underscored the potential legal and financial consequences of failing to adequately protect sensitive data and the importance of adhering to regulatory requirements to mitigate such risks.

The incident also raised important questions about the role of legacy software in modern IT environments and the challenges associated with maintaining and securing aging systems. Legacy software, often defined as older software that is no longer actively developed or supported, can pose significant security risks due to outdated technologies and vulnerabilities that may not be easily addressed. The Accellion FTA breach highlighted the need for organizations to regularly assess their use of legacy software and to prioritize the upgrade or replacement of outdated systems to ensure continued security and compliance with evolving security standards.

The breach also had significant implications for the cybersecurity industry, emphasizing the need for continuous innovation and improvement in security technologies and practices. The use of zero-day vulnerabilities by the attackers underscored the importance of proactive threat intelligence and vulnerability management to identify and address potential security weaknesses before they can be exploited. The incident also highlighted the critical role of collaboration and information sharing among cybersecurity professionals, vendors, and organizations to enhance collective defenses against emerging threats.

From a technological perspective, the Accellion FTA breach underscored the importance of adopting a layered security approach to protect sensitive data. Key elements of such an approach include the implementation of strong authentication mechanisms, such as multi-factor authentication (MFA), to prevent unauthorized access, as well as the use of encryption to protect data both in transit and at rest. Additionally, organizations are encouraged to implement advanced threat detection and response capabilities, such as intrusion detection systems (IDS) and security information and event management (SIEM) solutions, to monitor for suspicious activity and respond to potential threats in real time.

The breach also highlighted the importance of maintaining a strong incident response plan to effectively manage and mitigate the impact of data breaches and other security incidents. A robust incident response plan should include clear procedures for detecting and responding to security incidents, including the identification and containment of the breach, the investigation and remediation of vulnerabilities, and the communication with affected stakeholders. Organizations are encouraged to regularly test and update their incident response plans to ensure they are prepared to effectively handle potential security incidents and to minimize the impact on their operations and reputation.

The Accellion FTA breach also underscored the critical importance of data privacy and the need for organizations to adopt comprehensive data protection policies and practices. The exposure of sensitive personal and financial information highlighted the potential risks associated with the misuse of such data and the importance of implementing strong data protection measures to safeguard against unauthorized access and exploitation. Organizations are encouraged to adopt data minimization practices, limiting the collection and retention of personal data to what is necessary for their operations, and to implement data access controls to restrict access to sensitive information to authorized individuals only.

From an ethical standpoint, the breach raised important considerations regarding the responsibilities of organizations in protecting the privacy and security of their customers' data. The incident highlighted the need for transparency and accountability in the handling of personal information and the importance of building and maintaining trust with customers and stakeholders. Organizations are encouraged to adopt ethical data practices that prioritize the protection of personal information and to ensure that their data collection and use practices are transparent and aligned with user expectations.

Chapter 40: Log4Shell Vulnerability

The Log4Shell vulnerability, discovered in late 2021 and affecting systems well into 2022, represents one of the most critical and widespread security issues in recent years. Officially designated as CVE-2021-44228, this vulnerability resides in the widely-used Apache Log4j library, a Java-based logging utility incorporated into millions of applications and services worldwide. Its discovery sent shockwaves through the cybersecurity community, given the extensive use of Log4j in enterprise environments, cloud services, and consumer applications.

Log4j is an open-source logging library developed by the Apache Software Foundation. Logging is a crucial aspect of software development and maintenance, allowing developers to track the behavior of applications, diagnose issues, and monitor performance. Log4j's versatility and ease of use made it a popular choice for logging in Java applications, leading to its integration in a vast array of software systems.

The Log4Shell vulnerability exploits a flaw in Log4j's handling of log messages. Specifically, it allows attackers to execute arbitrary code on a server that uses the vulnerable version of Log4j. This is achieved through a process known as "log injection," where an attacker manipulates log messages to include malicious payloads. When these messages are processed by Log4j, the payload is executed, granting the attacker control over the system.

The exploit leverages Log4j's support for Java Naming and Directory Interface (JNDI) lookups. JNDI is a Java API that provides naming and directory functionality to Java applications, including the ability to look up data and services via various protocols. In Log4j, JNDI lookups could be triggered within log messages, enabling the inclusion of dynamic content. The vulnerability arises because Log4j does not adequately sanitize these lookups, allowing an attacker to craft a log message that triggers a JNDI lookup to a malicious server.

This server could then deliver a malicious Java object, leading to the execution of arbitrary code on the targeted server.

The implications of Log4Shell are profound due to the pervasiveness of Log4j. The vulnerability's ease of exploitation and the ubiquity of affected systems created a perfect storm, prompting widespread panic and an urgent response from the cybersecurity community. Organizations worldwide scrambled to identify affected systems and apply patches or mitigations.

The initial public disclosure of Log4Shell occurred on December 9, 2021, when a security researcher posted a proof-of-concept exploit on Twitter. This triggered immediate concern, as the simplicity of the exploit meant that even low-skill attackers could potentially leverage it. Within hours, the vulnerability was actively being exploited in the wild, with attackers scanning the internet for vulnerable systems and deploying a variety of malware, including ransomware and cryptojacking software.

Apache Software Foundation quickly released Log4j version 2.15.0 to address the vulnerability by disabling JNDI lookups by default and implementing additional safeguards. However, further scrutiny revealed that the initial patch was incomplete, leading to the release of subsequent versions (2.16.0 and later) to fully mitigate the issue. The rapid development and deployment of these patches underscored the severity of the situation and the need for organizations to remain vigilant and responsive.

The widespread impact of Log4Shell prompted coordinated efforts across the cybersecurity ecosystem. Government agencies, including the U.S. Cybersecurity and Infrastructure Security Agency (CISA), issued urgent alerts, advising organizations to prioritize patching and implement mitigations. Technology companies and cloud service providers, such as Microsoft, Amazon Web Services (AWS), and Google Cloud, worked to secure their platforms and assist customers in identifying and addressing vulnerabilities.

The fallout from Log4Shell highlighted several critical aspects of modern cybersecurity challenges. Firstly, it underscored the risks associated with third-party software components. As organizations increasingly rely on open-source libraries and frameworks, vulnerabilities in these dependencies can have far-reaching consequences. The incident emphasized the need for comprehensive software supply chain security, including rigorous vetting of third-party components and the ability to quickly respond to vulnerabilities.

Secondly, Log4Shell demonstrated the importance of proactive and layered defense strategies. While patching vulnerable systems is crucial, organizations must also employ additional security measures such as network segmentation, intrusion detection systems, and robust access controls to limit the impact of potential breaches. The use of runtime application self-protection (RASP) and web application firewalls (WAFs) can also provide additional layers of defense against exploitation attempts.

Furthermore, the incident highlighted the necessity of effective vulnerability management and incident response processes. Organizations with mature security programs were better positioned to quickly identify affected systems, deploy patches, and mitigate risks. This includes maintaining up-to-date asset inventories, employing automated vulnerability scanning tools, and having well-defined incident response playbooks.

The Log4Shell vulnerability also sparked discussions about the sustainability and security of open-source software. While open-source projects like Log4j benefit from community contributions and transparency, they also face challenges related to funding, resource allocation, and security oversight. The incident underscored the need for greater support and investment in open-source security initiatives, including funding for maintainers, improving code review processes, and developing tools for automated vulnerability detection and remediation.

In the aftermath of Log4Shell, there was a concerted effort to enhance the security of software supply chains. Initiatives such as the Open-Source Security Foundation (OpenSSF) and the Software Bill of Materials (SBOM) gained traction, aiming to improve the security and transparency of software components. These efforts seek to provide organizations with better visibility into their dependencies and enable more effective management of security risks.

From a regulatory perspective, Log4Shell reinforced the importance of cybersecurity compliance and reporting requirements. Governments and regulatory bodies around the world emphasized the need for timely vulnerability disclosure and response. In the United States, for example, the Federal Trade Commission (FTC) warned organizations about potential enforcement actions if they failed to address the vulnerability, highlighting the legal and regulatory implications of inadequate cybersecurity practices.

The impact of Log4Shell extended beyond immediate technical and operational challenges. It prompted a broader reassessment of cybersecurity priorities and strategies. Organizations recognized the need for a holistic approach to cybersecurity that encompasses not only technical defenses but also governance, risk management, and stakeholder engagement. This includes fostering a security-aware culture, investing in continuous security education and training, and building strong partnerships with external security experts and vendors.

Epilogue

As we reach the final pages of "Dark Digital Histories," we find ourselves at a crossroads in the ever-evolving landscape of cyberspace. The tales of cybercrime chronicled in this book have taken us on a journey through the dark alleys of the digital world, revealing the vulnerabilities and exploits that have shaped our modern existence. Each story, from the earliest worm to the most sophisticated state-sponsored hack, has left an indelible mark on the fabric of our interconnected society.

The cybercriminals and security experts featured in these chapters are more than just characters in a historical narrative. They are the architects and defenders of a digital domain that continues to expand and transform at an unprecedented pace. Their actions have forced us to confront the dual-edged nature of technological advancement—a force for progress that, if left unchecked, can also be a conduit for chaos.

As we reflect on the lessons learned from these dark digital histories, it becomes clear that the fight for cybersecurity is a perpetual one. The stories told here are not just about the past; they are warnings and guideposts for the future. They underscore the necessity of constant vigilance, innovation, and collaboration in the face of ever-more sophisticated threats.

In this digital age, where our lives are intertwined with technology, the stakes have never been higher. Personal data, financial systems, critical infrastructure, and even national security hinge on our ability to protect and defend against cyber adversaries. The cat-and-mouse game between hackers and defenders will undoubtedly continue, evolving with each new technological breakthrough.

However, there is hope. The same ingenuity that fuels cybercrime also drives the development of advanced security measures. The relentless pursuit of knowledge and the dedication of cybersecurity professionals worldwide offer a beacon of resilience and adaptability. Together, they form the front line in the battle to safeguard our digital future.

As we close this book, we are reminded that each of us has a role to play in this ongoing saga. Whether we are technologists, policymakers, educators, or everyday users, our actions and choices contribute to the security and integrity of the digital world. By fostering a culture of awareness, responsibility, and innovation, we can help build a safer and more secure cyberspace for generations to come.

"Dark Digital Histories" is not just a chronicle of crimes; it is a testament to the enduring human spirit in the face of adversity. It is a call to arms for all who value the promise and potential of the digital age. As we move forward, let us carry the lessons of these histories with us, ever mindful of the shadows that lurk in the digital expanse, and ever determined to illuminate and protect the path ahead.

The End.

www.ingramcontent.com/pod-product-compliance
Lightning Source LLC
LaVergne TN
LVHW010555160826
845677LV00013B/3136

* 9 7 9 8 2 2 4 7 7 5 0 7 1 *